E. F. (Ernst Friedrich) Richter, John P. tr Morgan

Richter's Manual of harmony

A practical guide to its study prepared especially for the Conservatory of Music at

Leipzig

E. F. (Ernst Friedrich) Richter, John P. tr Morgan

Richter's Manual of harmony
A practical guide to its study prepared especially for the Conservatory of Music at Leipzig

ISBN/EAN: 9783743312081

Hergestellt in Europa, USA, Kanada, Australien, Japan

Cover: Foto ©Thomas Meinert / pixelio.de

Manufactured and distributed by brebook publishing software (www.brebook.com)

E. F. (Ernst Friedrich) Richter, John P. tr Morgan

Richter's Manual of harmony

PRACTICAL GUIDE TO ITS STUDY

PREPARED ESPECIALLY FOR THE

CONSERVATORY OF MUSIC AT LEIPSIC.

BY

ERNST FRIEDRICH RICHTER,

UNIVERSITY MUSIC-DIRECTOR, ORGANIST OF THE CHURCH OF ST. NICOLAI, AND IN-
STRUCTOR IN THE CONSERVATORY OF MUSIC.

TRANSLATED FROM THE LATEST GERMAN EDITION

By JOHN P. MORGAN,

ALUMNUS OF THE LEIPSIC CONSERVATORY OF MUSIC, AND PUPIL OF THE AUTHOR.

SEVENTEENTH EDITION.

NEW YORK :

G. SCHIRMER,

1899.

TRANSLATOR'S PREFACE

In offering to the American public this translation of RICHTER's HARMONIELEHRE we need have no hesitation in saying, that we offer a translation of the best *text*-book of Harmony which has, as yet, been given to the world.

No one knows better than its author the road which one must take to become a *practical harmonist;* and no one has been more successful in leading pupils to real success.

The Manual contains the outlines of the course which has proved itself the best during his many years of efficient labor as Instructor in Harmony in the Conservatory of Leipsic ; and the immense sale the work has had in Europe, shows in what estimation it is held by the musical public.

A few remarks as to the translation :—Every one who is at all acquainted with the matter, knows how exceedingly difficult it is to do justice to a German scientific work in an English translation , and in no science is the poverty of exact and definite English terms greater than in that of music.

The translator has striven to give, throughout, the exact sense of the original, without any embellishment for the sake of attractiveness, and has always preferred a square-cut sentence containing the idea of the original *in full*, to a more smoothly-rounded one which would omit or add something.

A few clauses or words which seemed necessary for clearness, have been enclosed in square brackets.

The whole work has been performed as a pleasant duty to a

teacher to whom the translator owes all gratitude, and in behalf of the many earnest students in this country, who are utterly without an *adequate, practical* Manual of Harmony and Introduction to Counterpoint.

Thanks are especially due to his revered father, Rev. JOHN MORGAN, D. D., of Oberlin College, for his kind assistance in the work, which, without the aid of his comprehensive knowledge of language in general, and of the German in particular, must have been done much less accurately.

JOHN P. MORGAN.

NEW YORK, *June 1st,* 1867.

FROM THE PREFACE TO THE FIRST EDITION.

THE most immediate occasion for publishing this text book of harmony is indicated in the title. It was desirable, in connection with the practical course of studies in the theory of music, to put into the hands of the pupils a help for the explanation of the doctrines brought forward, and for their repetition. The qualities of such a manual, the author believes to be these: *It must contain the most essential, fundamental part of the musical theory expressed in a manner brief, but as complete as possible ; there must be these fundamental features always accompanied by reference and guidance to the practical application, in order to qualify for later attempts at composition.*

The book contains no scientifically theoretic treatise on harmony, but, although as far as is the case with any system of harmony, it is supported upon a firm basis, is only dedicated to the *practical* object, which with the scanty means now accessible would be very difficult to attain in an abstractly scientific way.

There has, indeed, ever been a disposition to inquire after a mathematical definiteness in musical rules, and especially youth, opposed to the belief in authority, would like to have everything so clear that no doubt would be possible, much as it shrinks on the other side, from learning, by means of the anatomical knife, to know and understand the blooming life of art ; and it is not to be denied that in this respect a want is found in musical literature, which no one has as yet entirely succeeded in supplying. All attempts

of the sort have as yet failed to create a really tenable scientifically musical system, according to which, through *one* fundamental
principle all phenomena in the musical realm are found exhibited
as always *necessary* consequences, and what philosophers, mathe-
maticians and physicists have accomplished in this regard, is
indeed worthy of attention, but in part, too much divided into
isolated portions to allow the easy discovery of the connecting
links for the completion of the whole, in part, too abstract, serving
music itself less than other objects, and with all the understanding
of musical things shown in it, still having little reference to the
properly musical, which is, after all, of the most immediate importance with the musician. What is laid down in musical
text books of a scientific basis, has not, however, hitherto verified
itself, because it in part as application of single learned investiga-
tions, was just as little able to create a system complete in itself,
with indubitable conclusions, and in part, as a fanciful structure,
was utterly without scientific basis. *

Still, rightly regarded, this deficiency is perceptible only to the
riper and educated musician, who likes to busy himself with theory,
not, however, so disadvantageous to the *advancing student of music*
that his immediate education must suffer in consequence of it; and
this scepticism, referred to above, might be compared in a certain
measure, with that childish mode of procedure, which from over
great curiosity, would get at the origin of all things through ques-
tions which seldom can be answered comprehensibly enough for
the questioner's stage of education. The advancing student of
music has to apply his whole power to his technical education,
because it will cost him time and trouble enough to attain the
stand-point, starting from which he can with greater ease advance
towards the position of a real artist. Here the question to be
asked is not *Why?* the inquiry of immediate application is, *How?*

---

* It may here be permitted to call attention to a work which might be adapted to
meet a palpable want: *Die Natur der Harmonie und Metrik by M. Hauptmann.*

The thing to be done is, from experience, from the best models, to understand, not to calculate, the necessity of certain principles : later, if education, acquirements, capability and calling require it, it will be time enough to investigate the *why*, and all knowledge obtained from experience will be an aid not to be despised, for discovering also the laws of nature pertaining to music.

This practical aim in view, the author was at pains to give the exhibition of harmony, and of the propositions resulting from observation and experience, in a simple and clear manner, and since he destined the book for *study*, to let the truths, perhaps contained in it, work through themselves ; without wishing, through an especially learned dress or an attractive form, to obtain for them an extended *circle of readers*. It contains the doctrine of harmony complete, with hints for a rational method of performing exercises, for the fixing of the whole, and for the ready carrying out of all harmonic principles. These exercises extend to the beginning of contrapuntal studies ; the doctrine of counterpoint itself will follow, however, in a later volume after the same plan.

In closing, still a word to the disciple of art ; an earnest one, indeed, but well meant.

It is our object to reach a distant goal ; this goal is the actual production of works of art. For this a vigorously exercised, enduring activity is necessary, to comprehend the musical principles, to form that which is won and recognized into structures capable of life. Those will bitterly deceive themselves, who, filled with the works of our great masters, gifted with a poetic mind, think to be able to pluck the blossoms, without learning thoroughly to know and prove the technical aids ; who are of the erroneous opinion that the consecration of beauty which extends itself over the work of art suffers under the dissection of the material, or that the first natural formations of the latter could never develop themselves to that requisite beauty. No person of talent has ever, without thorough knowledge (to attain which was, to be sure, easier to him than to the less gifted), risen to that height, upon which alone the achievements of art thrive. Exercise without consciousness is not artistic skill, it is only the working of the instinct, which will always make the want of a complete education sensible. The spiritual thought cannot do without the form, and it is this which must be recognized and learned. Even if it often comes with the conception of itself, still, with music, more than with anything else, it is of importance, as it were, logically to dissect the thought, to remodel it into new forms, to transform it in the most manifold manner. The knowledge of these things and skill in them must be acquired by the person of talent also, and this can only be attained by taking pains to recognize the musical laws, and endeavoring to imitate and extend what others have already long since discovered. Earnest, persevering activity, and above all, a rational method for the development of maturity, for the formation of works of art capable of life, will, in connection with musical capacity, certainly lead to the goal.

FROM THE PREFACE TO THE THIRD EDITION

ALTHOUGH in the present edition also, the methodical order of the former ones has been retained, still it has received material additions. The exercises for many subjects of instruction have been increased in number, where it seemed necessary.

As concerns the last, some books have appeared lately which are in a measure related to the present manual, viz: *Generalbass-Uebungen* nebst Kurzen Erläuterungen by BENEDICT WIDMANN, and *Uebungen zum Studium der Harmonie und des Contrapunktes*, by FERD. HILLER.

Although this is not the place to speak more particularly of these works, still let me here be permitted to thank these authors for their friendly reference to my work, and to make the following additional remarks in respect to it. Although the study of the theory of music through the so-called thorough-bass doctrine has long since yielded to a more rational method, still the thorough-bass figuring, as means to the end, has to me proved itself too excellent, to admit of my not using it for the first exercises in harmonic connections, as in general for the first applications of harmonic knowledge. A farther, more extended use of this has not been made in my text book itself, but in the first of the works above referred to, and, indeed, for exercises which, in part follow the course of my text book, in part aim at other practice. The work of HILLER, however, besides the exercises which professedly follow the course of my text book, offers in general a rich material for elaborations of the most manifold kind, not alone for harmonic exercises, but for all branches of theoretic musical education.

Since the exercises in my text book could not of course be exhaustive, and are, for the most part, given only in a suggestive way in order, when needed, to design others after them, both works may here be highly recommended for this object.

PREFACE TO THE FIFTH EDITION.

IT has been my endeavor in this fifth edition, also, which became necessary in a short time after the fourth, through additions, in part through altered verbal expression, to attain that perspicuity, which a text book of this kind must possess, if it fulfill its end completely. If I may also venture to hope that the book has been in many directions serviceable and of use, I am still conscious, that in order to reach the simple and luminous representation which is my ideal, many an improvement is still to be introduced. This edition, however, does not differ essentially from the preceding, and I wish, that beside the old friends, this new edition may gain for itself new ones.

ERNST FRIEDR. RICHTER.

LEIPSIC, *December*, 1863.

TABLE OF CONTENTS.

PART III.

PRACTICAL APPLICATION OF THE HARMONIES. THE EXERCISES IN THEIR USE IN THE PURE HARMONIC STRUCTURE.

JUST PUBLISHED! IN CONNECTION WITH THIS WORK:

ADDITIONAL EXERCISES BY ALFRED RICHTER.

Price, 50 cents net.

INTRODUCTION.

OF the elementary knowledge for which general instruction in music provides, and acquaintance with which must be presupposed at the beginning of the study of harmony, the portion which stands in the nearest relation to it, viz: *The Theory of Intervals*, will be treated of preliminarily in a brief and condensed manner.

Intervals.

The relation in which one tone stands to another, in respect to difference of pitch, is called *Interval*.

The greatness of the difference is directly determined according to the number of the degrees of the staff, upon which the two tones stand, in respect to each other, and, as a rule, in such a manner that the lowest tone is reckoned as standing upon the first degree, and the higher is determined according to the number of diatonic degrees lying between.

REMARK.—By diatonic degrees is understood the series or progression of tones presented by any major or minor scale.

If we take, for example, *g* as lower tone, and situated upon the first degree, then the *a*, being the higher, will come upon the second, the *e*, higher still, upon the sixth degree.

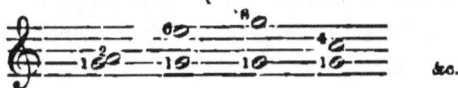

The numbers of the degrees produced thus, will be expressed in the following manner:

1	2	3	4	5	6	7	8
Unison or Prime.	Second.	Third.	Fourth.	Fifth.	Sixth.	Seventh.	Octave.

As a rule, we reckon only to the *octave*, and begin the series again with the tones which lie above, and so on with each new octave, so that the *ninth* degree becomes a *second*, the *tenth* a *third*, the *eleventh* a *fourth*, and so on; just so the fifteenth becomes the *octave*, the *sixteenth* the *second* again.

Reasons, however, which find their explanation in the principles of harmony and theory in general, give now and then occasion for designating tones which lie above the octave, according to the actual number of the degrees. The series of intervals from the octave upwards will, therefore, receive the following double designation:

Octave.   Ninth.   Tenth.   Eleventh.   Twelfth.   Thirteenth.   Fourteenth.   Fifteenth.

Second.   Third.   Fourth.   Fifth.   Sixth.   Seventh.   Octave.

Greater distances between two tones, are simply reduced to their relation in the lower octave.

More Particular Determination of the Intervals.

It is easy to see that the above presentation of the intervals, is based upon the diatonic major scale of C, and that the relations of the tones which lie between are not affected thereby. In like manner, they are regarded throughout, as based upon the *first* tone of the diatonic scale, whereas, it is conceivable that *any* tone of the scale can be taken at pleasure as lower tone, whereby the numbers of the degrees would be altered, and at the same time, small differences in the degrees themselves appear.

In order to gain a clear view of the matter, in the midst of these manifold variations, it will be well to note carefully the following principles:

The series of intervals shown above, in which the lowest tone is first tone of the major scale, which forms the series itself, serves as foundation for all determinations of intervals. These intervals are called MAJOR, *some of them* PERFECT.

Every chromatic alteration of these tones, of the upper tone as well as of the lower, not changing the number of the degrees, consequently does not alter their designation, but only renders a more particular determination of them necessary.

Thus, for example, if to the fifth $\frac{g}{c}$ a sharp is in any way attached, it remains always a *fifth*, but requires, however, a more particular determina-

tion, since it has evidently become a *different* fifth from what it was originally.

Or,

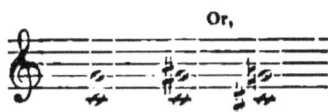

Since now such alterations of the intervals take place through chromatı-
cally raising or lowering them, the following various and more definitely
determinative designations are made use of:

1. *Seconds, thirds, sixths, sevenths* and *ninths*, which result from the
major scale, taking its *first* tone ior lower tone, are called MAJOR; *primes,
fourths, fifths* and *octaves* PERFECT.

2. If the upper tone of the *major* intervals be *lowered* a small half-step,
minor intervals result.

3. If the upper tone of [most] *major* and *perfect* intervals be *raised,* a
small half-step, *augmented* intervals result.

4. If the *lower* tone of most *perfect* and *minor* intervals be raised a
half-step, *diminished* intervals result.

To 1.

To 2.

To 3

To 4.

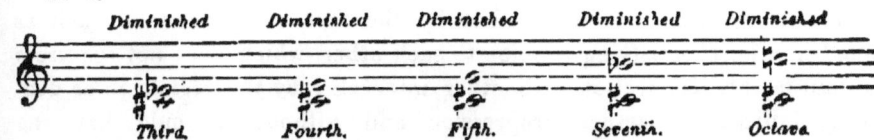

*Augmented thirds, sevenths and ninths do not occur in harmonic relations. Aug
mented octaves are to be regarded as augmented primes.

REMARK.—Diminished primes, seconds, sixths and ninths. are harmonically inconceivable, although they can be conceived of ir melodic relations, *i. e.,* in reference to *progressing* intervals, not to those which sound together.

Remark on the Formation of the Diminished Intervals.

The reason why, in the formation of the diminished intervals, the lower tone has been raised, notwithstanding that a like interval would result, if the upper tone were lowered, lies in the peculiar relations of all the intervals in regard to their inversion, which will be spoken of farther on.

General View and Classification of the Most Used Intervals.

Division of the Intervals into Consonances and Dissonances.

If we speak in music of consonant and dissonant intervals, we understand thereby, not well or ill sounding ones, which, to be sure, can be expressed by these two words, but by the first, we understand such as stand in a pure, satisfying relation to each other, which does not require a certain farther connection with other intervals; by the last, such as definitely indicate a farther progression, and without it would have no satisfying sense.

The *consonances* comprise all those intervals called *perfect* and, in addition, the *major* and *minor thirds* and *sixths.*

The first are called *complete* consonances, the 'ast *incomplete.*

The *dissonances* are the *major* and *minor second, major* and *minor seventh*, and all *augmented* and *diminished* intervals.

From this we derive the following general plan :

I. CONSONANCES.

a. Complete.

The perfect *prime*, perfect *fourth*, perfect *fifth* and perfect *octave.*

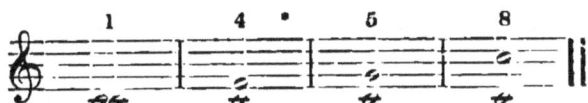

b. Incomplete.

The major and minor *third*, and the major and minor *sixth.*

II. DISSONANCES.

The augmented *prime*, the major, minor and augmented *second*, the diminished *third*, the augmented and diminished *fourth*, the augmented and diminished *fifth*, the augmented *sixth*, the major, minor and diminished *seventh*, the diminished *octave*, and the major and minor *ninth.*

---

*Later in the instruction in harmony, follows a farther explanation of the peculiar relations of the *fourth.*

Inversion (Versetzung) of the Intervals.

As was already indicated above, in determining the intervals we begin as a rule, with the lower tone. If, however, there is occasion to determine the relation of two tones, taking the upper tone as the starting point, the intervals found are called intervals *below*.

Thus, for example. [musical notation] is *d*, the fifth from *g ; g*, however, from *d* the fifth *below*. It is easy to see that the interval cannot be altered by this.

It becomes different, however, if the upper interval be *removed* below the original lower tone. Since particular reference is had to this inversion in various kinds of composition, an explanation of it may follow here.

The diatonic major scale will, by means of this inversion, assume the following form :

Intervals above: 1 2 3 4 5 6 7 8

[musical notation]

Intervals below : 8 7 6 5 4 3 2 1

There result thus, the following series of numbers :

1 2 3 4 5 6 7 8
8 7 6 5 4 3 2 1

that is, through inversion, the *prime* becomes an *octave*, the *second* a *seventh*, &c.

The inversion of the major scale forming the basis, we must note the following in respect to all intermediate intervals :

1. *All* PERFECT *intervals remain* PERFECT *in the inversion in the octave.*

2. *All* MAJOR *intervals become* MINOR, *all* MINOR MAJOR, *the* AUGMENTED D.MINISHED, *and the* DIMINISHED AUGMENTED.

In the following table is exhibited a view of all the inversions:

| | PRIMES. | | | SECONDS. | |
ORIGINAL INTERVALS.	Perfect.	Augmented.	Major.	Minor.	Augmented.
	[musical notation]				
	OCTAVES.			SEVENTHS.	
INVERSION	Perfect.	Diminished.	Minor.	Major.	Diminished.
	[musical notation]				

An exact, certain knowledge of this essential inversion of the intervals is not alone important for the exercises in double counterpoint, but greatly facilitates comprehension and insight, in simple harmonic structure, for which reason their study is urgently to be recommended.

A few more remarks may follow here:

The reason why, in the first table of intervals, (page 16), all *diminished* intervals were formed by raising the lower tone a small half step, and not by lowering the upper, is clearly to be seen from the above table of inversions. Since the *diminished* intervals result from the *augmented* through the inversion in the octave, this formation comes of itself; for example,

the augmented fourth must of necessity give the following dim-

inished fifth :

Just so the *perfect* fourth belongs originally to the consonances, since by inversion it is converted into the *perfect* fifth, in the same manner as the perfect fifth can only produce the perfect fourth, and never in any case does a dissonance result from the inversion of a consonance in the octave. Mention is made of this here because, in particular cases which are mentioned farther on, the fourth requires a similar treatment with some dissonances, which induced some theorists in earlier times, to explain it simply as a dissonance.

It will likewise be clear that the augmented octave, as also the ninth, cannot be inverted, since they never can become *intervals below.*

Other kinds of inversions, such as those in the tenth and twelfth, which produce entirely different results, may be passed over here, since they exercise no influence upon our next studies.

Since a complete and certain knowledge of all intervals is indispensable for the following harmonic studies, the practice of them in writing, as also an oral solution of given intervals, will facilitate much their correct comprehension,—which exercises are to be repeatedly employed.

HARMONY.

COMBINATIONS of simultaneous tones, formed from different intervals, according to certain fundamental principles, are called in general, *Harmonies. Chords.*

The doctrine of harmony makes us acquainted with the different species and kinds of chords, and shows their natural treatment. This consists in the *right* and *natural connection* of the chords among themselves, that is, in the transition, the resolution, the commingling of one chord into and with the following.

PART I.

THE FUNDAMENTAL HARMONIES AND THE CHORDS DERIVED FROM THEM.

Among the various kinds of chords which can serve for the harmonic foundation of a composition, those which present themselves as *independent*, without a definite connection with others, can be easily distinguished from those which indicate plainly a connection with other chords, and are therefore *not independent.*

To the first belong the most of the *triads*, to the last the *chords of the seventh.* These two kinds form the *fundamental harmonies*, from which all remaining chords are derived.

CHAPTER I.

The Triads of the Major Scale.

A *triad* is formed by a combination of three different tones. Of these, the lowest is called *fundamental* tone, to which its *third* and *fifth* are added, *e. g.*

These triads, formed upon *c, g* and *a,* present, however, a difference as to their intervals. While the triads of *c* and *g* are formed here by *major thirds* and *perfect fifths,* the triad of *a* contains a *minor third* and *perfect fifth.*

A triad with *major third* and *perfect fifth* is called a

MAJOR TRIAD

A riad with *minor third* and *perfect fifth* a

MINOR TRIAD.

Remark.—The explanation of other kinds of triads cannot follow until farther on.

As the diatonic scale makes up the content of a key, and forms the foundation of the melodic successions, so also the triads, which are founded upon the different steps of the scale, will form the essential part of the *harmonic* content.

Natural Connection of the Triads of a Key.

The triad which rests upon the first step of a key, is indeed the most important, the one which determines the key ; there stand, however, others in the *nearest* connection with it, which make clear its position.

In the natural presentation of the triad in thirds, the *lowest* tone shows itself as fundamental, the *fifth* as highest tone, and at the same time as ts culmination.

Each farther addition of a new interval would either alter the chord, or present tones already there, doubled. The next triad standing in connection with this must, to be sure, as an independent chord, lie outside its tone-mass, still, however, support itself upon one of its tones. This tone can only be found in the outer limits of the chord, viz : in *c* and *g*. G, which 's here the fifth, will thus form the *fundamental* of the one nearest standing triad, while *c* will in the same manner form the culmination, the *fifth* of the other, the fundamental of which would be F.

The connection of these three chords can be most plainly presented in the following manner :

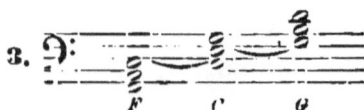

It is especially to be remarked of these three triads which stand in the closest connection, that their tones contain all the tones of the scale ; that they form the fundamental features of the key, and that they are, and must be those most frequently employed in practice, if the key is to p: esent itself clear and distinct.

On account of their importance also, especial names have been given to them. The one first found, standing upon the first degree of the scale, is called

THE TONIC TRIAD

The second, upon the fifth degree,

THE DOMINANT TRIAD

The third, upon the fourth degree,

THE SUB-DOMINANT TRIAD.

If we arrange these three chords according to their order in the scale, they present themselves to us thus :

and they show themselves collectively, as *major triads*

Application of the Harmonies Discovered.

In the application of these three, as well as of later chords, we avail ourselves of the *four-voiced* manner of writing.

REMARK.—The theoretical chord combination can be well presented, to be sure, three-voiced in manifold relation. It would, however, detain us longer from our practical aim, and may, for this reason, be reserved for a special presentation. The four-voiced movement will always maintain its importance as the foundation of all kinds of composition.

We regard, however, each harmony not as a mere mass, as compositions for the piano-forte often present them, but divide its component parts into *four different voices*.

The upper is called *Soprano,* the lowest *Bass,* these two together are called the *outer voices :* the voice next below the Soprano is called *Alto,* the one next above the Bass, *Tenor ;* these two together are called *middle-voices.*

The arrangement of these voices in the manner of a score is as follows, and the triad may be exhibited thus :

For the upper three voices especial clefs are used, which conform better to their compass than the above used violin [G] clef, and which will be spoken of later.

For our next exercises, we select for the sake of an easier view of the whole, not a separate staff for each voice, but will use the usual form of writing for the piano, (upon two staves).

The distribution of voices in No. 5, may be exhibited thus

6.

SOPRANO,
ALTO,
TENOR.

BASS

A twofold consideration of these various voices will take place : first in relation to the progression of each voice for itself alone, then in its relation to the remaining voices, both of which must be *pure* and *well-constructed*

The result of the fulfillment of these two conditions is called *pure lead ing of the voices.*

This *purity* of the harmony and its progression is attained through seeking out and practicing the *natural* and *legitimate* of harmonic combination.

Hereby arises the so-called *pure harmonic structure*, also called *strict style*, which prescribes rules and laws which proceed from the nature of music itself, the observance of which will afford the safest foundation for a later free use of the materials for composition. *By exercises in the pure harmonic structure is the judgment sharpened, the sense for the true and correct formed, and the taste purified.*

REMARK.—Inasmuch as every composition should exhibit self, through a correct use of all means at command and the *purity* resulting therefrom, (purity is here synonymous with natural expression), the term *pure harmonic structure* in a general sense, would require no farther explanation, as being a matter of course. In a more narrow sense, however, under *pure harmonic structure* we understand something farther, which is more nearly and better indicated by the expression of like meaning, *strict harmonic structure, strict style*, since this can be used in distinction to *free style*, whereas, properly speaking, no antithesis of the pure structure, such as, perhaps, *impure structure*, is to be assumed, since, as frequently as the latter in fact may occur, it were certainly to be designated as *false*, while the free structure might be essentially founded upon the *legitimate* of the pure structure.

As was indicated above, by *pure harmonic structure* is understood in a narrower sense such a one as in *the natural development of all tone relations, allows the fewest digressions from the legitimate, and only such as do not touch that which is essential, fundamental.*

If, in what precedes, the idea of pure harmonic structure is determined in a general way, still its boundaries are not yet drawn; and just this is a point which gives rise to th more difficulties for the beginner, as the boundaries are so very variously determined by the theorists themselves. This difficulty has occasioned many of them, especially some later ones, to omit entirely to speak of the pure construction, of the strict style; indeed to begin immediately with composition, and teach the laws of harmony from its inci dents. Whether this indulgence to youthful impatience, which does not willingly busy itself with the abstract, this inclination towards *premature* living creation, before the organic has developed itself to the capability for creation, can produce anything really *mature*, need not be further investigated here.

Let those who follow the views of this book and conform their studies to them, as also all who have to go through a *strict* school, be assured, that their freedom for future creation will by no means be lost by means of that which is *forbidden* to them, but will unfold itself so much the more fully, and with a more living power, upon a basis conformed to nature. The real mastery has ever been able to make itself apparent most genially within prescribed bounds, whereas the most lawless conceits frequently furnish proof of morbidity and weakness of mind. On the other hand, the pupil cannot be justified in making use of exceptions to given principles, which may perhaps be found in the works of the greatest masters, where the *rule* is concerned; or, in any case, to wish to produce compositions, when the thing to be done is to work out exercises theoretically well.

The three chords thus far known, being applied in the four-voice movement, will give occasion for remarks and observations, from which certain fundamental features and rules are to be established.

Since the triads only contain *three* tones, one component part (interval) thereof, must be doubled, if they are to be used in four-voiced writing.

Any Interval of the Triad can be Doubled.

The *fundamental*, however, usually presents itself as the tone most adapted for doubling, more rarely the fifth and third, and, indeed, the latter, in many cases which will be shown later, is not to be doubled at all

In order to accomplish the connection of two triads, the following rule is to be observed:

If a tone occurs in both of two chords which are to be connected, it is to be retained IN THE SAME VOICE, e. g.

In the Example *a*, C occurs in both triads as common tone; the Soprano which gave the first C, retains it also as fifth of the next chord. Just as in Example *b*, in which the G of the Alto affects the connection.

The remaining voices proceed to the tones which lie nearest to them, as at a the Alto from G to A, the Tenor from E to F, &c.

If in two chords no common tone appears, the voices are independently led in such a manner, that none appears with any other in PARALLEL FIFTHS *or* OCTAVES.

In order to explain this faulty progression more exactly, we must first make the necessary explanation of the movement of the voices in reference to each other.

The Relation of the Movement of the Voices in Respect to each other.

One voice can progress with another in

> Parallel [direct] motion (*motus rectus*),
> Contrary motion, (*motus contrarius*) and
> Oblique motion, (*motus obliquus*).

The *parallel motion* arises, if two voices rise or fall at the same time, *e. g.*

8.

They progress in *contrary motion* if the one rises and the other falls, *e. g.*

9.

The *oblique motion* arises, if, of two voices one remains upon the same tone while the other moves on, *e. g.*

10.

These three kinds of movement of the voices occur in chord connections in a *mixed manner.* Thus, in Example No. 7, *b,* the parallel motion shows itself between Soprano and Tenor, the contrary motion between Soprano, Tenor and Bass, and the oblique motion between the Alto and the remaining voices.

The above mentioned *faulty* movement of the voices in *parallel octaves* and *fifths,* can only appear in *parallel* motion: if, for example, two voices progress by degrees or skips in the following manner:

This *fault* is regarded as such for *all voices.*
The following connections of harmony contain both faults·

In Example *a,* are parallel octave skips between Soprano and Bass; in Example *b,* octave progressions between Alto and Bass, and in Example *c,* between Tenor and Bass. Parallel fifths are to be found in *a,* between Alto and Bass; in *b,* between Tenor and Bass, and in *c,* between Soprano and Tenor, as also at the same time between Soprano and Bass.

The best *means,* to avoid these and similar faulty progressions, is, for the above cases, *the use of the contrary and oblique movement of the voices;* that is, the voice which already forms an octave or fifth with another, must either move with it in *contrary motion,* or, if the following chord contains the same tone, remain stationary. The other voices then move on to the tones of the new harmony which lie nearest to them.

Thus in Example 12, *a* the oblique motion in respect to one voice, and at *b* and *c,* the contrary motion of all voices in respect to the Bass, is to be applied, *i. g.*

REMARK.—The reason for the *prohibition of octaves*, with which is con ected that o the progression in unison, can be easily found in the *necessary independence of the voices* It is more difficult to discover the ground for the prohibition of the *progression in fifths*, strong as the conviction may be of the necessity of it; and from the earliest times until now, much pains has been taken to express it clearly and definitely. On this point, let the following view be examined.

If each chord-formation presents for itself a separate *whole*, which, let it be formed as it may in other respects, is bounded mainly, as it were, by its fundamental and the fifth, as by a *circle*, (the seventh, as something additional cannot here be taken into account), and if the connections of harmony can only be produced by this: that one chord, so to speak, goes over into and resolves itself into the other; then it is evident that two chords with their boundaries, fifth after fifth, do not resolve themselves into each other, but, if they are placed side by side, will appear without relation to each other. This can be observed if we compare the following examples:

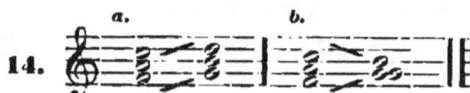

The sevenths, however, neither form, properly, new chords, nor do they lie, (according to the idea of a seventh), outside of the circle of the original chord, and only serve to indicate the relations of two chords, and to make the connections of the harmonies more intimate and firmer.

Everywhere now, where the *perfect* fifth appears, it will carry in itself its character of *boundary;* the remaining constituents of the chord, (as it were the content of the fifth), or anything additional, as the seventh, may lie above or below it; the unpleasantness of the succession of *two perfect fifths* will always be discoverable *in the deficiency in connection.*

Since we have spoken here of the fifths of the triads only, it may still be remarked, that in the case of *perfect* fifths which arise from added sevenths, the rule of their preparation, in part, to be sure, prevents parallel fifths, of itself; that, however, in the progression of one such seventh, which forms a perfect fifth with another voice, to a following perfect fifth, this last will cause the unpleasantness and deficiency of the connection to be heard, since this lies only in the *second* fifth, which enters without connection, *e. g.*

As concerns the diminished fifth, however, which in the dominant chord of the seventh can enter free under certain conditions, its free entrance even in the case of parallels, justifies completely the above expressed view, since, so soon as it appears *after* the perfect fifth, its connecting character makes itself felt, whereas, *before* the perfect fifth, leaving out on the account its farther laws of progression, the latter immediately steps *outside* of the circle of connection of both harmonies.

Compare the following examples,

If, however, instances of the following sort are frequently found in compositions of the stricter style:

we may assume that the doubling of the diminished fifth (the *f,*) requires a double progression of the same, and that the fifth-succession is thereby justified, because it lies in the middle voices; that, however, the following progression could not be called pure,

partly because they come forward too prominently in the upper voice; partly because the above condition of the necessary double progression is wanting, although instances such as No. 16. *c,* are often to be heard.

Hereby it becomes clear, also, why such parallel fifths as arise from passing notes, in many cases do not sound so unpleasant as those spoken of above, for which reason many theorists recognize them as faultless; which, at any rate, cannot be unconditionally admitted, since many of them are based upon other false voice-progressions. (for example, upon covered fifths), and it is not to be denied, that with a very open position and sufficient duration of the same, the unpleasantness of their operation becomes perceptible.

It is not the place here, to treat at greater length of these relations, and there would be much to say on many points; as for example, concerning the progression of the fifth of the augmented chord of the sixth and fifth, which would here carry us too far. Individual cases will bring us back to this point in connection with our practical exercises

If the sense of the foregoing representation should still be too obscure to the beginner, yet with more advanced knowledge, and exercises, and necessary frequent repetitions of the entire harmonic system, the comprehension of it will not long be wanting.

The faulty progression, thus far mentioned, is called *open fifth and octave progression*.

They are *covered*, if, in *parallel motion* of two voices, the *second* interval forms a *fifth* or *octave*, e. g.

19.

Open fifth and octave parallels remain, for harmonic combinations always inadmissible; the worth of *covered* fifths and octaves will be discussed farther on (in Chapter XVII.); for the present, this matter must be left to oral instruction, since, in general, with a *correct* comprehension of the exercises, not much opportunity will be offered for making unsuitable fifths and octaves.

REMARK.—The beginner will do well, in working out the first examples, to leave *covered* fifths and octaves entirely unnoticed, since, in a too anxious avoidance of them, frequently the first principles of chord-connection are violated, and other much worse faults easily arise. Much which follows will lead us back to this point, and with a more mature insight, the subject will be particularly discussed.

Exercises.

To bring musically into connection the three primary triads, with observance of the rules thus far established, will be the next exercise.

We select for this purpose the following Bass progression:

20.

REMARK.—These, as well as all subsequent exercises, give an indication in what way and manner our practical exercises will proceed. They are always to be continued as long as the point under consideration makes it necessary.

The situation of the upper three voices of the first chord, which are to be added, will yet give us occasion for important remarks.

---

* The figure over the Bass-note indicates the proper interval for the Soprano of the first chord.—ED

We have already seen in Example 5, that the situation of the voices in a
chord can be very different. This situation of the voices is called the
position of the chord.

Close and Open Position.

A chord appears in *close position,* if the upper three voices lie so near
to each other that neither the Soprano nor Tenor, if transposed an octave,
can appear between the two other voices, even if the Bass is somewhat
removed, *e. g.*

The first position of the chord *a* is in *b* so altered, that the former E of
the Tenor being placed an octave higher is given to the Soprano; in *c*, the
case is the same, with the two tones G and E; on the other hand, in *d*, the
C of the Soprano is placed an octave lower. In all these transpositions
the situation is indeed altered, but not the close position.

It is otherwise if the chord appears in *open* (also called *dispersed*) position, which is the case if either the Soprano can be placed between the
Alto and Tenor, or the Tenor between Alto and Soprano, so that thereby
the close position results, *e. g.*

At *a,* the chord appears in open position; by a transposition of the G
between the Alto and Soprano in close position *b;* just so at *c* and *d.* At *f*
the G of the Soprano of the chord *e,* is placed an octave lower between the
Alto and Tenor.

In this sense, however, the following situation of the voices (No. 23)
would not be open position, for by the transposition of the Tenor, the
situation of the upper voices would not be altered, *b,* and only the

transposition of the Soprano would produce the real open position of the chord, *c.*

23.

Even if the open position allows the chord to appear fuller, still it is not always to be applied, and, for our first exercises, is not clear enough to the view; so that we will for the present, write them in close position.

REMARK.—It will always be better in the beginning to work out the examples in close position, and only to use the open position later, from the examples of the second and third part onward, in which last they necessarily present themselves. In the beginning, the pupil, in the use of the open position, stumbles now and then upon difficulties, to overcome which cannot be our immediate object, and which had therefore better be evaded.

The various positions do not generally appear single, but occur combined, according as the leading of the voices requires.

If the position of the first chord is determined, the following chords are no longer so free, as to their position, that each can be chosen at pleasure, but it is regulated according to the rules for the connection of chords already given, pages 25 and 26.

This connection of chords and the leading of the voices of the first exercise, No. 20, may follow thus:

24.

C: I   V   I   IV   V   I

The natural relation of these chords to one another becomes clear by the above simple example, if we observe accurately their connection, especially, however, from the last two chords does the close connection, the mutual completing of one another, become plain. The feeling of return, of rest, of satisfaction, which lies in this connection of chords adapts them for forming the *close.* This form of close through the dominant chord, which resolved itself into the tonic triad, is called, if the latter falls upon the rythmical accent, *the authentic close.* [Cadence].

25.

V   I

Another form of close, which is formed by the subdominant triad, as above, No. 20, Example 4, is called the *plagal close.*

26.

IV   I

Of these and other kinds of close, we cannot speak more at length, until later

In order to become expert in writing the succession of chords which occurs if the Bass progresses by degrees, (as in Example 24, F—G), it will be to the purpose to write the successions IV–V and V–IV, in various positions and keys.

NOTE.—The expression *by degrees* is used here, as elsewhere in similar connection, to denote *from one degree to the next,* in distinction to *by skips,* viz., from one degree to another at a greater distance.—ED.

The Triads of the Remaining Degrees of the Major Scale.

All triads of the remaining degrees of a scale will, to be sure, belong to one and the same key, but will not indicate it so decisively as, for example, the combination of chords V–I.

These triads are called, to distinguish them from the primary triads,

SECONDARY TRIADS.

They are situated upon the second, third, sixth, and seventh degrees of the scale.

27.

II   III   VI   VII°

The triads of the second, third, and sixth degrees, appear as *minor triads,* since their *thirds are minor* and their *fifths perfect.*

The triad of the seventh degree is materially different from the others, because that, beside the minor third, it contains a *diminished fifth;* for this reason it is called the

DIMINISHED TRIAD

We select as an easy distinguishing sign, for the minor triad, a small numeral for the designation of the degree upon which it is situated, to which, in the case of the diminished triad, we add a 0, as above vii°, a manner of writing which the theorist, G. WEBER, has introduced.

All the triads of the major scale can now be exhibited thus:

28.

I   II   III   IV   V   VI   VII°

R<small>EMARK</small>.—The beginner must be very careful not to conceive of these chords, at their appearance, as all *tonic* triads, a misunderstanding which renders insight into harmonic combinations much more difficult. As long as C major is the ruling key, the triads of G, F, D. etc., are nothing else than *the chords of the various degrees of this key of C major, and belonging to it,* and no mention will be made of G major, F major, D minor so long as these keys do not appear as *independent.*

Hereby arises an ambiguity of the chords, which should be particularly noticed Each triad can belong to various keys. The major triad of C can be:

29.

C: I   F: V   G. IV

If, therefore, in respect to this chord, C major is spoken of (expressing the key in the general use of language), this is true only in the first case, if the C major triad occupies the *first* degree; in all other cases, however, it is incorrect

Application.

In the connection of these chords, as well among themselves as also with those found before, no new rule is at present necessary. Several things which are new will, however, appear in connection with it.

The Bass can move either *by skips* or *by degrees.**

In the first case there will always be connecting tones (like tones in two consecutive chords); in the last the progression of the voices must be in contrary motion, according to a rule mentioned above. (page 26), in order to bring out the inner connection of the chords.

---

* See Translator's note on page 33.

a. *The Bass progresses by skips*

30

As in this example, the skips in the Bass from the second degree have been treated, the same can be treated beginning from all other degrees, so that *tones common to the two chords always remain in the same voice.*

To this rule there are, however, in many cases, exceptions.

In Example 30, at NB., is found a progression of the voices formed according to the above rule, which contains an unpleasant covered octave between Tenor and Bass, and which is certainly improved by the following progression. Even if, in the last case, the *local connection of the tones* fails, still the *inner* connection is present, since the D of the Soprano in the first chord can easily be conceived as doubled through the lower octave, whereby the connection immediately becomes apparent, as in Example No. 31·

31.

REMARK —The reason, however, why exactly *this* tone should be conceived as double, since this could also be the case with any tone at pleasure, is founded upon the fact that it is the *fundamental*, the tone which gives to the whole chord its determination.

The unpleasantness of the covered octave mentioned, lies in the circumstance, that the upper voice progresses a *whole step*, and is yet more noticeable if it is contained in the outer voices, as in Example 32 at *a.*

32.

By the contrary motion of the Bass at *b*, the leading of the voices can be improved; in like manner, by the contrary motion in Example *c*, although here also a covered fifth shows itself between Soprano and Tenor (See the Remark on Example 34).

REMARK.—In the cases brought forward above. we do not speak of absolute faults It the leading of the voices is entirely given into our control, much can be avoided, which under other circumstances, for example, in the treatment of a *cantus firmus*, of a motive, or on other grounds important for the composition, is unavoidable. The improvement is here only presented from a theoretical stand-point. Concerning the covered fifth in No. 32 *c*, a farther explanation follows at No. 34.

The unpleasantness of the covered octaves spoken of ceases at once *if the upper voice progresses a* HALF STEP, *e. g.*

33.

b. *The Bass progresses by degrees.*

Here the contrary motion should always be applied, *e. g.*

34.

Remarks on these Chord-connections.

In all progressions of voices such as that used at NB. 1, and subsequent similar places, it is better to double the third of the second chord, in order to avoid covered fifths. Their unpleasantness is more noticeable if the chords appear in open position, *e. g.*

35.

The leading of the voices at *b* is to be preferred.

If these covered fifths occur in the middle voices, they are more allowable, because they are less perceptible.

36.

At NB. 2, the doubling of the third of the second chord is not always to be applied, since in general, the doubling of the seventh degree (in Example 34, the B of the second chord), is to be avoided.

Concerning the treatment of this tone, which is called *leading tone*, a fuller discussion will be given in connection with the following exercises

Exercises to be Worked Out.

37.

The fourth exercise gives occasion for a few remarks.

The progression of the Bass takes place here in the first four measures, in a regular, consequent manner. Such a regular harmonic or melodic progression is called *Sequence*.

This consequent progression of the Bass, occasions also a like regular leading of the remaining voices.

The treatment of this example, according to principles of chord-connection laid down above, by sustained tones, *e. g.*,

would not admit of the attainment of this end; the progression must rather follow in such a manner, that the chord of the second measure is brought into the same position which that of the first measure occupied, whereby the connecting tone D, does not remain in the same voice.

In the first example, on account of the sequence, the covered octaves spoken of above will likewise be allowable, if they are not found in outer voices.

In the third measure of Exercise No. 4, we meet with a chord, which thus far we have not used.

The Diminished Triad

It rests upon the seventh degree of the major scale, and is more dependent than the triads found thus far, since it plainly indicates a progression, which indication is effected by the dissonance, the diminished fifth.

The natural progression of the diminished intervals can in general be so conceived, that either both tones approach each other by a degree, (*a*), or the upper or lower tone progresses alone over against the other, (*b*, *c*), a kind of progression which only becomes plain through actual chord-connection.

The third following the diminished triad (*d*), exhibits the triad of the first degree (C) as incomplete, by omission of the fifth.

Since, according to the relations of the intervals in respect to inversion before explained, (page 18, 19,) an augmented fourth results from the diminished fifth, its progression must also appear in inverted order. See 40 *c*.

The fundamental tone upon which the diminished triad rests, is called

LEADING TONE.

It is found again as third in the dominant triad, and as fifth in the triad of the third degree.

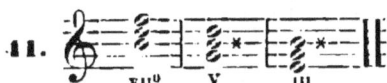

Since the LEADING TONE *of itself comes out very distinctly, it is* NOT DOUBLED *in the simply harmonic four-voiced movement.*

Just so its progression *one half step upwards* can be effected, if the next following chord contains this tone.

This tendency to progression lies in the melodic character of the leading tone, inasmuch as it stands as half-step before the fundamental tone of the scale. This is noticeable particularly in the case of the dominant triad, if the leading tone is contained in the upper voice, as *a* in Example 12. operates more satisfyingly, than *b* and *c*.

This inclination upwards shows itself less in the middle voices, as at *d*. Most intolerable in many cases, in such chord-connections, are skips in the upper voice (at *c*), whereas, on the contrary, skips in the middle voices (at *e*) are to be used, *if the Bass is led in contrary motion.*

In Example 39, third measure, is found a doubling and progression of the leading tone, *contrary to* the above rule. Both took place on account of the *sequence* contained in the example, which allowed no alteration of the position or the progression of the chord.

Concerning more Extended Formation of the Close.

The formation of the close through the chord of the dominant, noticed on page 32, (the authentic close), shows itself in a still more definite manner in the last examples.

As the natural relation of the chord of the dominant to the tonic triad, renders the two adapted to the formation of the close, so in these examples a still farther preparation of it is noticeable, through the triad of the second degree, which stands in the same relation to the chord of the dominant, in which the latter stands to the tonic triad, *e. g.*

43.

Besides the triad of the second degree, the triad of the sub-dominant is also adapted for this formation of the close, *e. g.*

44.

The *closing formulæ* (*cadences*) produced by this chord-connection, will assume more definite form through the application of the chords to be shown later.

CHAPTER II.

The Triads of the Minor Scale.

a. *Primary Triads.*

THE primary triads of the major scale were found upon the *first, fourth* and *fifth* degrees. Upon the *same degrees* we find also the *primary triads* of the *minor scale.*

The relation, however, in which the dominant triad stands to the tonic chord, that is, as it becomes plain through the formation of the close previously shown, renders the chromatic alteration of one tone of the minor scale necessary

Its *seventh tone-degree,* which, according to the signature of the minor scale, is always distant a whole step from the eighth degree, is chromatically raised a half-step, so that it acquires the character of a leading tone *e. g*

15.

By this means the formation of the dominant triad in minor, becomes exactly like that in major, thus:

46.

or briefly expressed:

The dominant triad in major and minor is always a major triad.

A comparison of the form of close of both modes shows this plainly

47.

That, however, the sixth degree of the minor scale is not, in a harmonic sense, capable of any such chromatic alteration by elevation a half-step, as is often necessary melodically, the plagal close proves *a* (see page 33), which cannot be conceived of at all as at *b*.

48.

The three primary triads in minor can be thus exhibited in their natural relation according to previous explanation ·

49.

The minor scale, as it forms the basis for the formation of harmonies will therefore b· the following :

REMARK.—All other forms of the minor scale, such as:

or descending ·

depend upon melodic conditions, which do not allow the *step of an augmented second* from the sixth to the seventh degree, found in No. 50.

These forms have no influence upon the harmonic formation in itself considered ; the harmonic foundation, however, has a reflex influence upon the minor scale itself, as the following examples show ·

&c.

The last case, in which the descending scale even exhibits the step of an augmented second B–A♭, which in future, in chord-connections we shall carefully avoid, explains itself thereby, that B was necessary as component part of the chord, A♭, however, in order not to destroy the minor character of the passage, which is done very perceptibly through A, while, in the ascending scale, (in the first example), this (minor character) is already perfectly secured through the minor third, E♭.

b. *The Triads of the Remaining Degrees of the Minor Scale.*

SECONDARY TRIADS.

After the establishment of the minor scale, the *secondary triads* appear in the following form :

The *second* degree gives a *diminished* triad, as before the seventh degree of the major scale; in like manner a *diminished* triad is found upon the *seventh* degree. The *sixth* degree forms here a *major* triad.

The *third* degree exhibits a new form of the triad.

It contains a major third and an augmented fifth, and is therefore called

THE AUGMENTED TRIAD.

The constrained or forced character of the connection of this chord with other chords of the same key, allows it seldom to appear *as fundamental harmony of the third degree* of the minor scale. The following examples may serve to prove this:

Of these examples, those under *c* and *e* will be best adapted for use. The introduction of this chord shows itself to be more difficult still.

Its introduction is most tolerable, if the augmented fifth is prepared, that is, exists already in the same voice as constituent part of the preceding chord, (at *d*).

REMARK.—There is something peculiarly foreign in the chord of the third degree, as well of the major as of the minor scale, so that this harmony, even when it appears simply as minor triad in the major scale, is very difficult to connect naturally and effectively with other chords, and therefore seldom occurs.

Most of the practicable chord-connections exhibited above will occur in other relations, and not allow the augmented triad to be recognized as [triad of the] *third degree of the minor scale.* The augmented triad, which is much used in the later music, belongs to the *chromatically altered harmonies,* which will be explained later under the name *Altered Chords.* (See Chap. X, Altered Chords).

Application.

The principles of the connection of harmonies and leading of the voices, already developed, will also have application here, and particularl in the connection of the fundamental chords in minor, what was said about the progression of the leading tone comes very distinctly into view since the step of an augmented second, occurring in the minor scale between the sixth and seventh degrees, as well as descending, between the seventh and sixth, is to be avoided as *unmelodious*, if both tones, which contain the step of an augmented second, *belong to different harmonies, e. g*

57.

Hence, in the often recurring connection of the chords of the fifth and sixth degrees, the progression of the leading tone will be necessarily always upwards, whereby, in the triad of the sixth degree *the third appear doubled, e. g.*

58.

Thus, it would not be possible to exhibit in a correct form the example given under No. 57 *b,* unless we make use of a mediating tone, such as, for example:

59.

REMARK.—The practice deviates, in certain and especial cases, from this rule. It will be well, however to accustom ourselves to the leading of the voices above shown, and the more, as we must not overlook the fact, that *every deviation from the rules in the practice is and should be only a well founded exception*, whereas the observance of the rule can be instanced in numberless cases.

Exercises in connecting the Triads of the Minor Scale.

80.

Remarks on these Exercises.

A chromatic sign over a Bass note *without a figure*, as, for example, in the third measure of the first exercise, refers always to the *third* of the Bass. This raising of the third in the dominant triad, which occurs very often in minor, is the raising of the leading tone spoken of, (page 40).

The triad is, as a rule, not marked in the thorough-bass notation, if the Bass contains the fundamental, unless especial reasons exist for indicating t by 3, 5, 8, or $\frac{5}{3}$ or in full, by $\frac{8}{5}{3}$

One reason for indicating it by 5, is found in the third and sixth exercises. Here the introduction of the triad of the third degree in minor has been attempted, whereby it was necessary to indicate that the fifth is raised, since it likewise forms the seventh degree of the minor scale.

The figure 3 or 5 over the first chord of some of the examples, indicates its position. See, in regard to this, the remarks to the next exercises, (page 50).

The working out of an exercise will confirm the fundamental feature hitherto developed. We select for this purpose the first exercise.

61

The first principle of the connection of chords (by connection of tones in the same voice), is here everywhere observed, and for this reason the

Alto, in the third measure (at NB.), makes the faulty step of an augmented second from F to G♯.

In order to avoid this fault (according to page 44), it will be necessary to let the Alto progress from F to E, and to lead the Soprano from B to G♯, while the Tenor skips from D to B, in the following manner·

62.

(a connection of chords, which has already been explained in No. 31 where the connection of tones does not take place in the same voice), or the Soprano retains the B and the Tenor goes from D downward to the G♯, the Alto from F to E, whereby the close position is forsaken, and this and the following harmony appear in open position:

63.

Farther remarks, which the difficulties in the leading of the voices in reference to the chords of the fourth, fifth and sixth degrees of the minor scale render necessary, are in especial cases to be left to practical guidance.

Before we proceed to the farther use of the triads, we will exhibit, in the following manner the chords hitherto discovered:

View of all Triads of the Major and Minor Scales.

64.

Major triads are found

Minor triads

Diminished triads

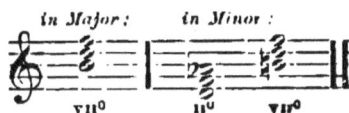

Augmented triad

CHAPTER III.

The Inversions of the Triads.

The Chord of the Sixth, the Chord of the Sixth and Fourth.

The appplication of the triads, and indeed of all fundamental chords, is not limited to that use of them in which the *fundamental* lies in the *Bass*, as in all previous examples; the Bass can also receive the *third* or *fifth* of the fundamental chord. Hereby arise transformations of the fundamental chords, which are called

INVERSIONS

of the chord.

REMARK.—It should be well remarked, that only *transpositions of the Bass* to another interval are here spoken of, and that the before mentioned transpositions of the other voices into close and open position, and to various intervals, *by no means essentially alter the chord.**

Two of the inversions are possible with the triad:

a. *If the Bass receives the third of the triad, there arises the* CHORD OF THE SIXTH.

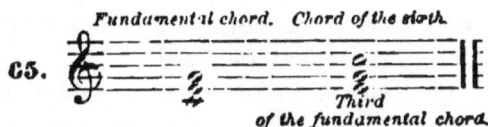

65.

Fundamental chord.   Chord of the sixth.

Third of the fundamental chord.

---

* The word *transposition* is here used in its *general*, not its *technical* sense. —ED.

b. *If the Bass receives the fifth of the triad, there arises the* CHORD OF THE SIXTH AND FOURTH.

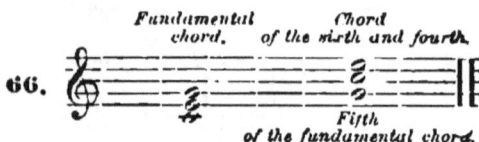

66.

The chord of the sixth is indicated by 6 over the Bass note, that of the sixth and fourth, by $\frac{6}{4}$; *e. g.*

67.

The letter shall in future serve for indicating the fundamental tone, and, as before, the numeral to indicate the degree, whereby, as can be seen in Example 67, only the *situation of the fundamental tone* can be taken into consideration, not, however, the casual Bass.

REMARK.—As the fundamental tone of the *chords of the sixth* and *of the sixth and fourth* in Example 67, is always C, and not the Bass notes E and G, so the chord itself will not lie upon the third or fifth, but upon the *first* degree, since, in fact, these are *no newly formed chords*, but only chords brought into another position by the Bass, and therefore *derived chords*.

Every triad can appear in such inversions.

Application.

By the use of the inversions of the chords, not only does the leading of the harmony receive more variety, but the movement of the voices, and particularly of the Bass, becomes thereby more flowing.

According to the above noticed rules for the doubling of an interval of the triad (page 25), it will also be better in the case of the chord of the sixth, in the four-voiced movement, to double the *fundamental* of the *original chord,* and the doubling of the Bass tone in the chord of the sixth (that is, the original third), can take place *only if the natural leading of the voices* requires it, or if thereby certain faults can be avoided. That the leading tone, even if it lies *in the Bass,* is to be excluded from this doubling, may be yet remarked after what was said on page 39.

Just so, it needs merely to be mentioned, that the position of the upper three voices is conditioned only by the leading of the voices, and aside from this, has no essential influence upon the chord itself.

The *chord of the sixth* can therefore occur in the following forms:

68.

The use of the *chord of the sixth and fourth* is more rare than that of the *chord of the sixth*, and requires certain conditions which shall be mentioned later. We meet it oftenest in the formations of the close. The *Bass tone*, the fifth of the original chord, is best adapted for doubling, and the chord will appear in the following and similar forms:

69.

In the connection of these chords with others, no farther mechanical rules are necessary beyond those already given; we likewise omit the mere mechanical combination of two or three chords, and show the application of these derived chords in small pieces of music, which, however insignificant, still contain the image of a whole, whereby individual cases can be better judged of in relation to the whole.

Exercises.

70.

Remarks on these Exercises.

The indication of the fifth in the first measure of the second Example, as also all similar indications in the future, denote the situation of the Soprano, and therewith the position of the first chord. If no figure stands over the first Bass note, it is to be assumed, that the Soprano can best receive the octave of the Bass.

The *diminished triad* appears in the second exercise as *chord of the sixth.* It occurs oftenest in this situation. It may here be called to mind that its fundamental tone is not doubled, because of its being the *leading tone,* whereas, in most cases, the third (in the *chord of the sixth* the Bass tone) is doubled. The leading of the voices occasions, sometimes, also a doubling of the fifth.

The progression of the diminished triad is always conditioned by the leading of the Bass. The natural direction of the diminished triad in its fundamental position is already given, page 38.

In the most usual cases the progression of the Bass is as follows:

and the progression of the remaining voices thus:

It is evident from the above Examples, that the inversion of the diminished fifth, viz., the augmented fourth, will not necessarily, in *four-voiced movement*, have the same progression as was given above, *two-voiced*, pag 38. We see, in the first example and others, B and F of the Soprano an Alto progress to C and G.

73.

The similarity of this chord, in sound, to the dominant chord of the seventh to be shown later, often induces beginners to lead the diminished fifth *downwards*, even if it has converted itself by inversion into the augmented fourth; this, as the above examples show, is necessary *only* in case it really lies *above* the fundamental as diminished fifth, and a progression of the following sort:

74.

is faulty on account of the parallel fifths.

REMARK—It may yet be remarked here, that parallel fifths, of which the one fifth is diminished and the other perfect, are to be allowed *if the diminished follows the perfect fifth, but not vice versa*, e. g.

75.

Compare also the Remark, page 28.

The progression of the voices takes another form in the diminished triad, if the Bass goes over to a chord, other than the tonic triad. A few chord-connections may follow here:

76.

The diminished triad of the second degree in Minor allows another treatment, since its fundamental can be doubled.

The succession of *two* or more *chords of the sixth*, with a progression of the Bass by degrees, as in Exercise 70, No. 3, and others, will render necessary one or more voices moving in contrary motion to the Bass, *e. g.*

The series of chords of the sixth of the 5th and 6th Exercises in No. 70 can, to be sure, be carried out in various ways; best, however if the consequent succession of the Bass is retained also in the remaining voices, *e. g*

Covered octaves, as in the 2d and 3d measures between Tenor and **Bass** re not to be avoided in such cases. It can be deduced from this, *that to* SINGLE *progressions of the voices which are contrary to rule, that especial importance is not to be attached,* IN OPPOSITION TO THE CONSEQUENCE OF THE WHOLE, *which otherwise belongs to them,* since the construction of the

details, although it must be as perfect as possible, will always be su. ordi-
nate to that of the whole.

REMARK.—It is not to be ignored, that the principle laid down above can easily b
misunderstood by the beginner; however, the laying down of the principle was not t
be evaded, and it may be added here, in order to avoid possible error, that a decision in
these things, in the last instance, belongs only to a judgment fully matured by expe
rience and practice.

Concerning the Signs of the Thorough-Bass Notation.

The numbers and signs of the Thorough-Bass are called in general *sig
natures*, [in German works *Signaturen.*—ED.] Some of them have
already been explained, as the chromatic sign occurring very often in minor.
The notation of the chords of the sixth and of the sixth and fourth was
given, page 48. A stroke through the figure is used, (for example, in the
Exercises 8, 9, 10, of No. 70, a stroke through the 6 : ♯), if a chromatic
elevation of the interval a half-step becomes necessary; instead of which,
however, a ♯ or ♮ is often set after the figure (*e. g.*, 6♯ or 6♮. 5♮.) Other
figures will find their explanation later in connection with the chords
which they concern.

Formation of the Close through the Chord of the Sixth and Fourth.

In the Exercises of No. 70 we see, through the inversion of the triad.
the formation of the close previously mentioned, extended and put into a
much more definite shape. We discover, namely, that the chord of the
sixth and fourth of the tonic triad, coming before the dominant triad, indicates decidedly the close.

79.

C: I   V   I

The chord of the sixth and fourth is frequently preceded by the triad
of the fourth or second degree.

80

C: IV   I   V   I   II   I   V   I

As decidedly now as the chord of the sixth and fourth indicates the close, having also a decided influence in the modulation into foreign keys, just so weak is the effect of its entrance under other relations, so that its proper use is subject to certain conditions, which will be treated of later.

CHAPTER IV.

Harmonies of the Seventh (*Vierklänge*).

The harmonies of the seventh are founded upon the triads. They result from the addition of a third to the fifth of the triad, which [third] forms a seventh from the fundamental.

Not only the various kinds of triads, but also the various kinds of sevenths will afford manifold harmonies of the seventh.

The General Properties of the Chords of the Seventh.

The chords of the seventh are not so independent as the most of the triads, but indicate definitely a progression, so that they *never alone,* but only *in connection with triads,* afford anything complete or finished. On the other hand, they will render the relations of the chords to each other closer and more intimate, and by means of this quality furnish in particular excellent means for the connection of chords and for the leading of the voices.

The Dominant Chord of the Seventh in Major and Minor.

The chord of the seventh which is most important, and occurs oftenest is the

DOMINANT CHORD OF THE SEVENTH,

also called *primary chord of the seventh.*

It rests, like the dominant triad, upon the fifth degree, and is formed *zactly alike* in major and minor, that is, *from the major triad and minor seventh.*

In the fundamental position it is marked by a 7 over the Bass note, and in our method of notation, indicated by V_7

83.

The relation in which the triad of the dominant stands to the tonic triad, has become clear principally through the formation of the close shown before, (see page 33). The close will come out still more clearly through the use of the dominant chord of the seventh.

The following combination of chords will show the formation of the close:

84.

REMARK.—It is to be remarked here, that the triad following the chord of the seventh is incomplete; in both cases the fifth of the triad is wanting. The reason of this will appear from what follows.

The striving after a point of rest, inherent in these chords, and the resulting union with a triad, is called

RESOLUTION OF THE CHORD OF THE SEVENTH, (*Cadence*).

If the union of the dominant chord of the seventh with the tonic triad follows in the manner exhibited in No. 84, or in a similar way, it is called

CLOSING CADENCE.

For the leading of the voices, the progression of the intervals of the chord of the seventh will furnish important observations.

We observe first the closing cadence as the *regular* resolution of the dominant chord of the seventh especially.

The seventh, as the essential interval of the chord, is, by its relation to the fundamental, confined to a definite progression. If the progression of the Bass, which contains the fundamental, is regarded as given, an upward progression of the seventh will appear impossible:

85.

even if, as at *b,* a third voice is added ; whereas its downward progression affords full satisfaction :

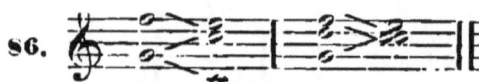

86.

Since the progression of the *fundamental* by an upward step of a fourth or downward step of a fifth is already determined, the progression of the *third* and *fifth* of the chord of the seventh remains to be considered.

The third of the dominant chord of the seventh is always the leading tone of the scale; its natural direction is therefore determined by what has been said before concerning the leading tone, (page 39); its progression will follow a half-step upwards, and *b* will, therefore, not appear so natural as *a* :

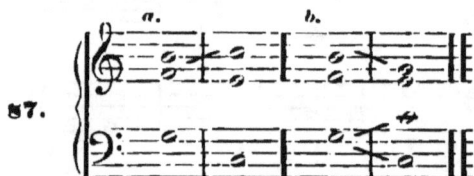

87.

In the Example 87, *b,* the third, is given to the upper voice, which render the unpleasantness of its progression quite perceptible.   This leading becomes tolerable if the third is found in a middle voice, *e. g.*

88.

This downward leading of the third (leading tone) is therefore to be applied under the following conditions :

1.   *If it does not lie in the upper, but in a middle voice, e. g.*

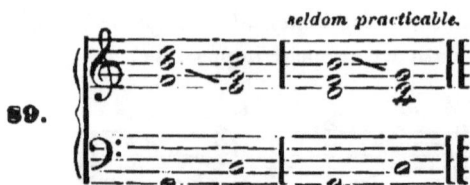

seldom practicable.

89.

b *If the Bass progresses in contrary motion, e. g.*

90.

The reason of the second rule becomes evident, if we observe the covered fifths in the last Example *b,* between Alto and Bass.

The leading of the *fifth* of the chord of the seventh is free. While, for the most part, it is crowded a degree downwards by the seventh, reasons may exist connected with the leading of the voices, for allowing it to progress a degree upwards, as Example 88 *b* shows, where the D of the Soprano is lead to the E.

If we condense these remarks, we find the following rules for the regular resolution of the chord of the seventh, and for the closing cadence in particular :

The seventh progresses a diatonic degree downwards, while
The fundamental makes a skip of a fourth upwards or a fifth downwards ;
Just so the third is led a degree upwards toward the seventh, while
The fifth can be led by degrees, upward or downward.

REMARK.—By the progression of the *third towards the seventh*, we are reminded of what was said of the fundamental and the diminished fifth in the diminished triad, (page 38). Both intervals are found again in the dominant chord of the seventh.

Application.

Except in the formation of the closes, the dominant chord of the seventh is, in the middle of a piece, seldom employed *in the usage thus far known to us*, and, if it does take place, only in a position whereby the feeling of the complete close is not produced.

This takes place particularly in cases where the seventh of the chord lies in the upper voice, whereby the close becomes incomplete, or, if the dominant chord of the seventh falls upon the accented part of the measure (thesis), since in the complete close (cadence) the tonic triad must fall there. (See page 33).

Besides this, the chord often appears incomplete through the omission of an interval. This interval, however, can only be the *fifth*, seldom the *third*, while the omission of the fundamental or the seventh, would entirely alter the chord and render it incapable of recognition.

In *a, b, d,* the fifth is omitted, in *c,* the third, and in each case
the fundamental doubled instead, which doubling affords, by means of the
tone which is allowed to remain stationary, the closest connection with the
following chord, and allows the tonic triad to appear again complete,
which was not the case in the previous resolution.   (See No. 84).

We add the following remark upon the omission of an interval in the
chord :

*Through the leading of the voices a chord can appear incomplete; the
omitted interval will, in most cases, be the fifth of the fundamental chord.*

Exercises.

These exercises require no farther explanation.   It has been already
mentioned, that the chord of the seventh, in the position known to us now

is indicated by 7, also that the sharp found under it, or in general, all chromatic signs which occur without figures opposite to them, have reference to the third from the Bass tone.   (See page 55.)

CHAPTER V.

The Inversions of the Chord of the Seventh.

LIKE the triad, the chord of the seventh can be altered in such a manner, that the Bass receives an interval other than the fundamental.

The first inversion arises, if the Bass receives the third of the fundamental;

The second, if the fifth of the fundamental chord lies in the Bass, and

The third, if the original seventh is given to the lower voice.

In close position the inversions present themselves thus:

A comparison of these inversions of the chord of the seventh, with those of the triad, shows plainly their analogous position:

These derived chords receive their designation from the position of their intervals:

The *first* inversion is called the *chord of the sixth and fifth.*

The second: the *chord of the sixth, fourth, and third,* or briefly, *chord of the fourth and third.*

The third: the *chord of the sixth, fourth, and second,* or briefly, *chord of the second.*

Their designation in the Thorough-Bass notation is to be seen above, in Example 94.

It needs only to be remembered here, that in these inversions, just as before in the inversions of the triad, only the position of the Bass or of the lowest voice is essential, and that the remaining intervals can be variously distributed among the upper voices, *e. g.*

95.

Application.

The regular progression (resolution) of these derived chords is founded upon that of the fundamental chord.

If, in its case, the *dissonance*, the seventh, conditioned the progression in one direction, the tendency to the same progression (resolution), will also exist in the case of the derived chords, in which the two tones, the fundamental and the seventh, either appear again, or become seconds by inversion.

96.

Progression of the Chord of the Sixth and Fifth.

Since the original *seventh* shows itself likewise, over against the Bass tone in the chord of the sixth and fifth, as *dissonance*, as *diminished fifth*, the progression of which was discussed above, (page 38),

97.

the resolution of the chord of the sixth and fifth will naturally take place thus :

98.

The progression of the fundamental, as before given, does not appear here, since the G of the upper voice is sustained and transforms itself into the fifth. This is, however, only apparent, for that it forms the foundation of this connection of harmony, the marking below G₇ C, of Example 98 proves.

That however, the Soprano, or a middle voice, cannot in notes carry out the progression of the fundamental in such cases, lies, beside other reasons, immediately in the character of these voices, which is to be found more in mediation and connection of the harmonics, than in laying their foundation, which belongs to the Bass.

REMARK.—Deviating progressions of the fundamental in these cases, such as a freer leading of the voices in certain relations would give, are not hereby excluded, only there must be an inner connection of the chords.

Progression of the Chord of the Sixth, Fourth, and Third.

We find again here, beside the seventh and its inversion, the diminished fifth or its inversion, the augmented fourth:

The resolution of this chord follows thus:

The Bass, the original fifth, can progress in both of the given ways.

Progression of the Chord of the Second.

This chord has the peculiarity, that the original dissonant intervals, the *seventh* and the *diminished fifth*, can only occur in their inversions, as *second below*, and *augmented fourth below*.

The progression of this chord is as follows:

Thus the resolution of the *chord of the second* is effected here through the *chord of the sixth.*

We can perceive in these resolutions, that they are all based upon the natural progression of the dominant chord of the seventh, which before

was called *cadence*, for we find everywhere the same marking of the fundamental G₇ C or V₇ I.

These resolutions will, therefore, themselves form *cadences*, only not o.
so complete a sort as those mentioned above, and as those are called *perfect
cadences*, so these are designated by the name, *imperfect cadences*.

*View of the Natural Progression of all Inversions of the Dom-
inant Chord of the Seventh in various positions.*

a. The Chord of the Sixth and Fifth.

b. The Chord of the Sixth, Fourth, and Third

c. The Chord of the Second.

Exercises in the Use of these Chords.

OBSERVATION.—The marking 8 7 in the next to the last measure of the second, fourth, and fifth Examples, denotes that the seventh should not appear with the chord itself, but follow after the octave.

CHAPTER VI.

Secondary Harmonies of the Seventh.

WHILE in the case of the triads, *three primary chords* are requisite to establish the key, (the relation to the tonic triad as central point), there is needed in the case of the chords of the seventh, only *one primary chord, the dominant chord of the seventh*, the content of which alone already renders the key certain, and the natural progression of which to the tonic triad represents the key.

REMARK.—The manifest fact, that the seventh of the dominant chord of the seventh is at the same time *fundamental* of the subdominant triad, renders the relation of the two tones G and F, (as fundamentals of the dominant triads), to their common centre, C, (as tonic triad), already entirely clear. (See above, page 22. 3).

Beside this dominant chord of the seventh, also called *primary or essential chord of the seventh*, harmonies of the seventh can be formed from the remaining triads in major and minor, the relation of which to a definite key is indeed undeniable, but by no means so decided as in the case of the primary chord. They are called

SECONDARY CHORDS OF THE SEVENTH.

They are to be formed, simply by the addition of a *seventh of the fundamental* to the triads:

We come here to chord formations, which, in part, without connection with other chords, sound very harsh, and, for this reason, foreign, because, as was already remarked above, their relation to a *fundamental key* is not so decided and clear as that of the dominant chord of the seventh. Their use will, therefore, be in part more rare, but not the less adapted for imparting variety and especial coloring to the harmonic succession.

Among these secondary chords of the seventh, the following kinds may be distinguished:

a. *Major triads with major seventh.* **105.**

in Major: *in Minor:*
C: I₇ IV₇   A: VI₇

NB. *Major triads with minor seventh always form dominant chords of the seventh.*

b. *Minor triad with major seventh.*

in Minor: not used as fundamental harmony.
A: I₇

c. *Minor triads with minor seventh.*

in Major: *in Minor:*
C: II₇ III₇ VI₇ A: IV₇

d. *Diminished triads with minor seventh.*

in Major: *in Minor*
C: VII°₇ A: II°₇

e. *Diminished triad with diminished seventh.*

in Minor:
A: VII°₇

f. *The augmented triad with major seventh,*

A: III'₇

as it is found upon the third degree in minor, is, to be sure, not useless, but from reasons before developed in the case of the augmented triad, is very seldom used, and ambiguous.

REMARK.—We find this chord again, with another foundation, in Chapter X.

Application of the Secondary Chords of the Seventh in Major.

The *seventh* or its inversion, the *second*, may be major, minor, diminished, or (which concerns the second only) *augmented;* it will always in its relation to the fundamental press as dissonance to a progression.

This *natural progression* is, with the secondary chords of the seventh, no other *than that already found in case of the dominant chord of the seventh,* viz., *one degree downwards* toward the fundamental, if the latter moves by fifths or fourths, downward or upward.

If accordingly the progression of the principal intervals of the chord is found,

106.

for the remaining intervals, no new rule is necessary; the *third* will be led *one degree upward*, while the progression of the *fifth* can be in either direction.

107.

REMARK.—The deviation from this rule in the progression   the third in Example 107 *b,* is occasioned by the circumstance, that the covered octave, which would appear in the regular *ascension* of the *third* a *whole step, e. g.,*

108.

was avoided thereby.   See page 35, Example 32.

Whether, however, as in Example 107 *c,* the leading tone should be doubled in the succeeding chord, or the following covered fifths be preferred,

109.

will depend upon circumstances which can only be judged of in the application to particular cases.

Natural (Cadencing) Progression of the Secondary Chords of the Seventh in Major.

a. of the first degree.

110.

with omission of the fifth:

b. of the second degree.   *or:*

C: II₇   *not:*   *not:*

without fifth:

not:

c. of the third degree: *without fifth:*

not: *not:*   *not:*   *not:*
C: III₇   VI

d. of the fourth degree (seldom with this resolution).

not good:

not: *not:*
C: IV₇   VII

without fifth:

not:

e. of the sixt. degree.   *without 4 th:*

not: *not:*   *not:*   *not:*

C: vi₇   II

f. of the seventh degree.   *not good:*   *better:*

not:

C: vii°₇   III

without fifth:

not:

REMARK.—The above found progressions of all chords of the seventh are neither in their positions exhaustive, nor have they been exhibited as the only possible ones.

The difficulty of forming such progressions lies only in the frequently occurring covered fifths and octaves. All the remarks also, which are added above, such as "*not*," "*not good*," which, for the most part, refer to the leading of the Bass, (inasmuch as this, with other necessary voice-progressions, produces these faults,) are, in many cases, only to be understood from a *theoretical stand point*, while such cases and similar ones in the practice, even in the so-called pure harmonic structure, must often be judged according to the principle before expressed, (pages 52 and 53).

Since the theory has not yet succeeded in furnishing *positive rules* for all cases of the kind, the true and false, the admissible and inadmissible in this respect, can only be distinguished by means of *complete harmonic education* and a *really musically educated ear.* More about this follows later.

Concerning the especial Progression of the Chord of the Seventh of the seventh Degree.

In the above found collection of the progressions of all chords of the seventh in major, under No. 110, that of the *seventh degree,* analogous with the others, has been led to the *third degree,* that is, the progression of the fundamental takes place, as with the other chords of the seventh, through a step of a fourth upward or a fifth downward. This progression is the more unusual one, and is, for the most part, only used in a leading of the harmony according to a certain formula (sequence). That progression occurs oftener, upon which the *diminished triad*, to which here the seventh is added, is based, (see page 38 and 50), viz., that to the tonic triad.

The above Example shows plainly, that the relation of the *diminished triad* to the *tonic triad* is not altered by the addition of the seventh, but on the contrary, becomes more decided.

It is likewise to be remarked, that, if the chord appears in the above position, the *third* of the following triad must be doubled, (see No. 111 *b*), because otherwise, perfect fifths would arise; (See No. 112 *a*),

or a skip must be used, as at *b,* a leading of the Tenor which is often found, and which, in spite of the covered octave, is very effective.

It is peculiar to this chord, that only that position of it in which the *seventh* lies in the *upper voice* produces a satisfactory effect, while the other positions, if not impracticable, still appear less clear.

REMARK.--Whether the reason of this is, that in the seventh with its above used progression, the character of the ninth lies, (as some theorists assert, that the dominant chord of the seventh, with added ninth, is the basis of this chord with its resolution), which, though similar to that of the seventh, is still much more comprehensive, and does not bear the situation in the middle, cannot here be further investigated.

The Freer Treatment of the Third and Fifth in the Chord of the Seventh.

Various progressions of these intervals have already been used in the previous connections of chords. The *fifth* goes upwards and downwards, the *third* likewise, sometimes goes a degree upwards, and sometimes makes a skip of a third downwards. This all took place principally in reference to, and in avoidance of, covered fifths and octaves.

Where these faulty progressions do not interfere, the *third* especially, can make still other steps, by means of which the leading of the voices often becomes more independent and freer, *e. g.*

That this leading is also possible in the middle voices, if the position admits of it, is shown at *c.*

The leading of the Soprano at *b* is not good, because a *skip of an augmented fourth* occurs in consequence.

The skip from the *fourth* to the *seventh* degree, (F–B), is called the **Tritonus,** because it contains three whole steps. More of this subsequently.

A different leading of the fifth is possible only if the Bass at the same time deviates from the above progression, which is that of a fundamental: as in general, still other leading of the voices will present itself, if we search out other than the chord-connections hitherto used.

The Preparation of the Seventh.

Thus far the progression of the chords of the seventh has been spoken of, but nothing has been said of their *introduction*

The harsh effect of the entrance of many *dissonances,* and particularly of most of the *sevenths in the secondary chords of the seventh,* renders necessary a careful introduction of them, which consists in their *preparation.*

A tone is prepared, *if it exists already in the foregoing chord* IN ONE AND THE SAME VOICE, *and as harmonic tone,* so that it can be connected by a tie.

Such preparation of a tone is contained already in the *first* connections of chords previously shown, *e. g.*

115.

It can be said here, that C of the Soprano in the second chord is *prepared* by the C of the first chord; likewise the G of the Alto in the Example following.

The *necessity* of the preparation of the sevenths, however, does not result alone from the harsh effect of their entrance if they are struck *free*, [enter unprepared], but particularly from the *character of* harmonic *connection* and *binding* of two consecutive chords, which is especially characteristic of the sevenths, and which, without the preparation, would not appear.

The *preparation of the seventh* can now take place in the following manner:

116.

In all these Examples, the tone which is connected by a tie with the following like tone, forms the *preparation of the seventh*.

In the formation of such preparation, the following rules are to be observed:

a. *The preparation takes place upon the unaccented part of the measure* (arsis) and must

b. *at least, be of as long duration as the succeeding seventh;* it can indeed be longer but not shorter. *e. g.*

REMARK —*The preparation of the sevenths* forms one of the most important parts of the doctrine of harmony, and is to be carried through and practiced with much care, because upon it rests the most essential part of the inner and most intimate connection of harmony.

If *here* also exceptions in the practice can be adduced, we may still again be reminded, that they are even nothing else than *exceptions*, which prove nothing against the importance of the principle of harmonic connection, but can only be intended and judged of as called for in a concrete case by the position and relations. (Page 44—Remark).

These exceptions occur mostly with the *minor sevenths*, as the less harsh, as those of the second and seventh degree, and are then always softened by good leading of the voices.

An especial exception, however, to the necessary preparation is formed by the *seventh of the dominant chord*, also called the *essential seventh* This is the one, which, through its relation to the tonic triad, enters [with an effect] the least harsh and foreign to the fundamental key, and does not require preparation in all cases.

Of its farther use the following may be remarked

The dominant seventh does not, to be sure, require preparation, yet its free entrance demands the presence of the fundamental, if the leading of the voices is to be pure and without harshness.

REMARK.—The so-called *passing sevenths*, which of course, as such, cannot be prepared, conform to the rules of the passing notes, which are explained later Concerning the passing sevenths, see Chapter XVIII.

The seventh also of the seventh degree in major and minor (in the last case, the chord of the diminished seventh), by reason of their especial character do not by any means always require a preparation.

Exercises.

The Connection of the Chords of the Seventh among themselves.

The *progression* or *resolution* of the chords of the seventh, took place in the former Examples, always through the *triad of the fourth degree above*, or, which is equivalent, *of the fifth degree below.* Instead of the triad, a *chord of the seventh* of the same degree can also follow.

The progression of the voices suffers hereby no alteration, only, in this case the *third* of the first chord of the seventh will serve as the necessary *preparation of the following seventh*, and will therefore not progress, but remain stationary, *e. g.*

Here the *third* of the dominant chord, the B, forms the preparation of the following seventh.

The peculiarity in this connection of harmony is, that in *one of th* chords of the seventh, the *fifth* will always *be wanting.* In Example 120, the fifth of the first chord has been left out. If several chords of the seventh succeed each other, the *fifth* will always be wanting in each *alternate* chord.

The following rule may therefore apply for connections of harmony of this kind :

If two or more chords of the seventh follow each other IN THE FUNDA MENTAL POSITION, *the fifth is omitted in each alternate chord.*

Exercises.

Application of the Secondary Chords of the Seventh in Minor

The use of the *secondary chords of the seventh in minor* is more lim ited. Many of them show themselves, to be incapable, or indefinite and ambiguous, for chord-connections as they were applied in major, others form, in their cadencing progressions, heavy, unmelodic steps of the voices.

A *chord of the seventh* formed as the *first* degree gives it, can afford no progression analogous to the above, since the following chord connection is not conceivable.

REMARK.—Even if with the above *combination of intervals*, progress; as can I s formed, such as perhaps:

124.

still this would hardly be admissible as proof that we have in this a progression of t chord of the seventh of the first degree in minor.

The resolution of the chord of the *second* degree is into the *dominant* and is very frequently used.

125.

a: II°7   V   *not:*   *not:*   &c.

A progression of the chord of the seventh of the *third* degree is not impossible,

126.

a: III'7   VI   *not:*   *not:*

it is *ambiguous*, however, and might be better adapted to C major than to A minor. (See *Altered Chords*).

It may be remarked here, in addition, that the *fifth* in this chord, as *augmented interval*, will always go *upward* one degree.

The chords of the *fourth* and *sixth* degrees are unusual, because the leading of the voices in their resolution becomes inconvenient and unmelodi.

127.

a: IV7   VII°   *good:*

128

A: VI₇ II⁰

The forced character of most of the above progressions is unmistakable, and prevents their frequent use.

The *seventh* degree in minor brings an important chord, which is generally known under the name of

THE CHORD OF THE DIMINISHED SEVENTH.

A resolution of this chord in the manner of all the rest is impossible, since it would necessarily result in the triad of the third degree, which was already represented above as doubtful and ambiguous.

Instead of this, its progression, *as with the chord of the seventh of the seventh degree in major* (see page 68), is based upon the *natural progression of the leading tone*, upon which this chord rests:

129.   A: VII⁰₇ I   α: VII⁰₇ I

As the *fundamental* of this chord (leading tone), progresses a *half-step*, so the *seventh* also moves a *half-step* downwards, while *third* and *fifth* are led just as regularly as with the other chords of the seventh; especially, however, in many positions (No. 130 *a*) must the leading of the *third* be accurately attended to, because it easily produces faulty progression:

130.   *a.*   not: *b.*   *c.*

whereas the position at *b* and *c* gives to the third greater freedom.

REMARK.—The natural progression of this chord, as well as of the chord of the seventh of the seventh degree in major, to the tonic, has occasioned the older teachers of harmony to find the basis of it in the *dominant harmony of the seventh.* They conceived of this chord with a ninth (major or minor) added to it, and the fundamental omitted whereby arose both chords of the seventh degree.

While we refer to that which is said later (in Chapter IX.) of the chord of the ninth we can only bring forward here as reason for the view offered, that this assumptic 1 of the cherd of the ninth is needless and far-fetched, and that for practical purposes, the simplicity of the harmonic system has been preferred to the more excursive explanation of it.

For the application of the chord of the diminished seventh, observe in addition the following:

The diminished seventh, as the mildest of all, *needs no preparation* (See page 72).

Exercises.

The foregoing and al. previous exercises of this chapter, which, of course, only have the object to assist us in learning to use *mechanically* the chords thus far explained, and to test the rules and remarks laid down, have something inflexible and stiff in their structure, because the great number of chords of the seventh could only appear here in the *fundamental position* and because the introduction of many of them upon our present stand point, which did not allow us the selection of other means, was difficult, and could only appear forced.

What follows may serve as explanation of them:

The *fundamental* of these chords of the seventh makes everywhere the cadencing skip of a *fourth* or *fifth*, as is to be seen from the leading of the Bass, only, in the third exercise of Nos. 122 and 131, there is found, seemingly, an exception. In the fourth measure of the third exercise of No. 122, the *Bass tone,* to be sure, remains stationary, the progression of the fundamental is, however, contained in a perfectly regular manner in the two chords: A_7, D_7. The Bass tone could here remain stationary, because we have already learned the *inversions of the dominant chord of the seventh,* and can therefore use them. The case is the same in the fifth measure of the third exercise of No. 131, where the progression of the fundamental A₇–D takes place with a stationary Bass.

In the second Exercise of No. 131 the *chord of the seventh of the third degree in minor* is used, and, it may be assumed, that with this introduction it will not appear unnatural and harsh.

CHAPTER VII.

The Inversions of the Secondary Chords of the Seventh.

THROUGH the inversions of the secondary chords of the seventh *the same derived chords arise*, which have already shown themselves before with the dominant seventh, viz., the *chord of the sixth and fifth*, of the *sixth, fourth and third,* and of the *second.*

The variousness of the third, fifth and seventh of the fundamental harmony occasions no alteration in the treatment of the inversions. For although the *major* seventh changes, through inversion, into a *minor* second, and the *diminished* into an *augmented*, still its progression will ensue in the same manner as has already been explained above.

132.

There is need of no new rule for the progression of all these chords of the seventh. Only, that of the *seventh degree* in *major* and *minor* requires, as was before remarked, a little caution on account of the easily occurring *open fifths*.

Somewhat more concerning their treatment may follow here.

Progression of the Chord of the Seventh of the Seventh Degree in Major.

133.

All these inversions of the chord may be used, only the last, the chord of the second, will most seldom be in place, since the resolution into the chord of the sixth and fourth could only occur in rare cases, and at most as *passing chord.*

We must not allow ourselves to be misled in respect to their usefulness by the crowded position in which these chords are exhibited in No 133. It is only important, as was mentioned before, whether the seventh comes to lie *above* or *below* the fundamental (see page 69), and positions of the chords of the sixth and fifth, and of the fourth and third of the following sort,

134.

appear more satisfying, because the seventh lies *above* the fundamental.

The *chord of the diminished seventh* requires a manner of progression similar to the foregoing *e. g.*

135.

That here likewise the *third* inversion, the chord of the second, will be that least adapted for use, is shown by the unsatisfying resolution into the chord of the sixth and fourth, a chord which always requires a careful treatment, concerning which chord, what is necessary follows later.

That successions of fifths, which arise through resolution of the chords of the sixth and fifth, and of the fourth and third, in this manner:

136.

are to be regarded as faulty, has been already mentioned above, (page 76). Concerning the succession of this sort of fifths, compare also page 29, Nos. 16, 17, and 18.

With this exceedingly pliant chord, the position of the fundamental as respects the seventh produces no such material difference, as with the chord of the seventh degree in major; the seventh can lie *above* or *below* the fundamental, the similarity of sound of the augmented second to the minor third, will always impart much mildness to the chord and cause *the former* only to be felt as such in reference to the key

Exercises.

CHAPTER VIII.

The Chords of the Seventh in connection with Chords of the various tone-degrees other than those thus far used. Deceptive Cadences.

THE known rule, that the seventh must, in the resolution, progress one degree *downwards*, verifies itself, to be sure, completely, in the connections of chords previously shown, but it has as little *positive* authority as any thing else which, under other conditions, and in the great variousness of chord connections, is subject to necessary alterations.

In the movement of the *seventh* or of its inversion, the *second*, everything depends upon the progression of the *fundamental*. If this is of such sort, as in all the cases hitherto shown, that without the downward progression of the seventh no *intelligible* and *satisfying result* would be produced, then also the above rule will have full application.

The progression of the fundamental, however, can entirely set aside this direction of the seventh; it can either *remain stationary* or even *progress upwards, e. g.*

This leads us to the possibility of connecting the chords of the seventh with chords of tone-degrees, *other* than those hitherto used. A few known kinds of chord-connections now follow with remarks, in order to be able, in attempts at new formations of the kind, to proceed according to critical principles.

We begin with the *dominant chord of the seventh.*

It has been mentioned before, that the resolution of the chords of the seventh in the manner hitherto used is called *cadence,* and that of the dominant chord of the seventh *closing cadence.*

If any chord other than the tonic triad follows the dominant chord of the seventh, the natural inclination to a close is either *delayed* or entirely *set aside.*

The expectation of the natural succession experiences hereby a disappointment, and for this reason these connections of chords are called

DECEPTIVE CADENCES.

Deceptive cadences arise thus everywhere, where the progression of the dominant chord of the seventh does not result in the tonic triad, but lead, to *other chords.*

Some varieties of them will next be explained.

1. *The connection of the dominant chord of the seventh with triads other than that of the tonic, with a progression of the seventh by degrees downwards.*

a. *Connection with the sixth degree.*

139. C: V₇ VI   A: V₇ VI

This chord-connection (deceptive cadence) occurs very frequently.

The effect of this progression is not so decided with the *inversions* of the chord of the seventh, and is therefore more rare:

140. C: V₇ VI   A: V₇ VI

b. *Connection with the third degree.*

141. C: V₇ III

REMARK.—The attempts with the inversions of the chord are omitted here and in what follows; they are easily made.

This progression becomes more decided under the application of *modulation:*

142. C: V₇ A: V

The connection with the triad of the *third* degree is also possible in minor, but this as dissonant chord (through the augmented fifth) will make a farther succession necessary.

143. A: V₇ III' VI

2 *The connection with triads, the seventh remaining stationary.*

a. *With the second degree.*

not: impracticable in Minor.

144.

C: V_7 II   —   A: V_7 II^0

b. *With the fourth degree.*

In Major: In Minor:

145.

C: V_7 IV   A: V_7 IV   —

The connection of the dominant chord of the seventh with *harmonies of the seventh* of other degrees beside those before used, is likewise possible. A few of them follow here:

6th Degree: 3d Degree: or: Minor: 3d Degree.

116.

C: V_7 VI$_7$ V_7 III$_7$ V_7 A: V_7 A: V_7 III'$_7$ VI

If we modulate into other keys, the possibility of new connections extends itself greatly, e. g.

a. *With a downward progression of the seventh.*

not: better:

147.

C: V_7 D: V_7 —   C: V_7 B: VII$^0_7$ A: V_7 F: V_7 A: V_7 G: VII^0

b. *The seventh remaining stationary.*

148.

C: V_7 E♭: V_7 C: V_7 B♭: V_7 A: V_7 C: V_7 A: V_7 G: V_7

3. *The connection of the chords through an upward progression of the seventh.*

This case can occur with the common cadence (V—I).

a. *With an exchange of the progression of various voices.*

119.

Through the step of a third, of the Bass, the downward progression of the seventh becomes impossible, since the covered octave occurring thereby

150.

is in any case faulty.

In the remaining voices this progression of the fundamental cannot be introduced.

151.

All these Examples are faulty.

b. *The fundamental remaining stationary:*

152.

The fundamental serves here as so-called *stationary voice.* (See later: Organ point). It must however lie *at a distance* from the seventh, and the following progression would be faulty:

153.

c. *Through chromatic alteration and with modulation.*

154.

C: V₇ G: V₇

enharmonic:

C: V₇   G: V₇   V₇ E: vii°₇   C: V₇ F♯: V₇

d. *Through contrary motion of the Bass with modulation into other keys*

155.

C: V₇ D: V₇   C: V₇ B♭: vii°₇ A: V₇ D: vii°₇   C: V₇ F: V₇

(See above, No. 149.)

The foregoing catalogue of chord-connections gives only an indication of possible combinations. The object of them was to call attention to the manifoldness of harmonic progression and its capability for construction.

Concerning the *worth* of these and similar chord-combinations, criticism can only decide in *especial cases*, since their right use becomes possible only with a proper attention to their *introduction*, their *succession*, their *rythmical weight ;* in short, their whole situation.

The particular character of a piece of music, the peculiarly formed leading of the voices through the application of a motive or thought, and the like, can lead to such combinations of harmony ; to apply them, however, upon speculation, to produce new and strange forms in any case, in order to appear original, would probably in few instances so succeed, that the intention would not be apparent.

Exercises.

156.

REMARK.—The *open* position of the 5th exercise has reference to a leading of the voices adduced page 84; farther on, it can be abandoned again.

The Secondary Harmonies of the Seventh Connected with Chords of other Tone-Degrees or Keys.

A few more connections of chords with secondary chords of the seventh may here follow. To adduce all cases of the kind would be as impossible as it would be without object.

a. *With regular progression of the seventh.*

b. *With free progression of the seventh.*

158.

C: II$_7$ G: V$_7$ C: II$_7$ o: VII°$_7$ C: II$_7$ A: V$_7$ C: II$_7$ D: VII°$_7$

REMARK.—The reason why the last example is not good, lies in the so called *cross relations* therein found, the explanation of which follows later.

c. *The seventh remaining stationary.*

159.

C: II$_7$ IV   II$_7$ VI   II$_7$ I   II$_7$ I   V

The last chord-succession is often used. It forms a delay of the cadencing progression of the second degree to the fifth, through the inserted chord of the sixth and fourth of the tonic triad. Its chord of the sixth also often appears between this chord and its resolution, as in Example **c.**

The *chord of the diminished seventh* is often used in like manner:

160.

o: VII°$_7$ C: I   V

Here also the natural progression is only delayed through the chord of the sixth and fourth.

The mechanical combination of such chord-successions may be left to personal practice and investigation. The *advantage* of it will lie in the insight gained into the relations of chords, and therefore is not to be esteemed so insignificant as it might at first appear; this [practice] will, in fact, stand in about the same relation to composition, as the technical studies and preparatory exercises, to the practical bringing out and representation of musical works. Both produce aptness and skill, educate the powers, and render intellectual productions possible.

It may here only be remarked in addition, that the *relation of the seventh to the fundamental and its progression* must always be regarded as the criterion of the above combination. If this is pure and the remaining voices form none of the before mentioned faults, then the chord-combination can be used for particular cases.

Exercises.

161.

REMARK.—Many of the cases above adduced could not be taken up in these exercises, because they are based upon modulation, which is not particularly explained until later. (The sixth exercise makes a little application of modulation.) Many of the above Examples would also have become smoother and less stiff and strange, by the application of modulation.

CHAPTER IX.

On Chords of the Ninth, Eleventh and Thirteenth.

In most text-books are found extended discussions respecting these chord-formations.

The views which can be plausibly maintained respecting them are various, and will lead to the same *practical* result. We can assume

Either that this combination of intervals is to be regarded and treated as *real chords;*

Or, that they, as *unessential chord-formations,* either belong to the *sus pensions,* or arise *accidentally* on account of a voice remaining stationary.

In the first case, the explanation of their use, especially through their inversions, becomes very extended; and also obscure, (since in the four voiced movement one or more of their tones or intervals must be omitted, because they are then easily mistaken for other chords.

In the second case their explanation becomes much more simple.

REMARK.—The chords of the ninth, as well as those afterwards named, are a relic of the old so-called thorough-bass doctrine, which was fond of conceiving of every combination of tones, however accidental it might be, as an especial chord and taught its treatment, without arranging the many chance chord-phenomena under a definite system, and thereby made the whole doctrine of harmony much more difficult and diffuse.

Without being able here to enter into the theoretic reasons which class this kind of formations with the *accidental ones,* the possible *simplification of the harmonic system* without real practical disadvantages, determines us at once to the last view. (More respecting this in Part II.)

In order to gain a clear view, the formation of these unessential chord will be shown, and remarks added.

If we add a *ninth* to the dominant chord of the seventh, a chord arises, which is known under the name of the *dominant chord of the seventh and ninth.*

In major we find the *major,* in minor the *minor* ninth.

This chord is used in the pure harmonic structure, as in similar relations the dominant chord of the seventh itself, with preparation of the *ninth* or of the *fundamental;* and cases of the following sort, where *both tones* enter free

are to be consured on account of their stiffness and want of connection

This preparation can be effected thus:

161.

How far the first examples are to be reckoned as belonging to the suspensions, and the last to other accidental chord-formations, cannot be explained until later, in Part II.

REMARK.—From the chord of the ninth in major they derive the *chord of the seventh of the seventh degree,* which we have treated of fully before; likewise the *chord of the diminished seventh* from the chord of the ninth in minor, in order to be able to form their cadencing progression in a manner analogous to that of the other chords of the seventh, since it is said, that these chords are themselves *dominant chords of the seventh,* to which the ninth is added, and the fundamental of which is omitted, *e. g.*

165.   C: V₇ V₇ I   c: V₇ V₇ I

Through this arises, with the first, the complication that we must accept of *two* chords of the seventh of the seventh degree in major; one, the natural cadence of which is the following:

166.

the other as derived from the dominant chord of the seventh, while it remains the simplest way to refer to the character of the leading tone upon which the above chords rest.

That many musical text-books accept also of *secondary chords of the seventh and ninth,* renders the explanation of many harmonic formations still more complicated, and is just as little necessary, since none of these tones are to be introduced without preparation, whereby, in their whole treatment and succession, they differ in no respect from the *suspensions.*

That which, according to the practice, as well as according to a more simplified theory, applies to the chords of the ninth, will apply in still greater measure to the *chords of the eleventh* and those of the *thirteenth.*

The strange and frightful form of these chords is the following:

167.

In the pure four-voiced movement they can, of course, never be applied, since, through the necessary omission of many intervals, they will appear simply as suspensions, *e. g.*,

168.

and even in the polyphonic movement they will not distinguish themselves at all, in their character, from the suspensions; in the more free style, where they also appear without preparation, they can be regarded as *changing notes.*

CHAPTER X.

Chromatic Alteration of the Fundamental Harmonies. Altered Chords.

THE *chromatic alteration* of one or several intervals of the fundamental harmonies has a double effect:

Either *it produces a modulation,*

Or, *it gives to the chord a new formation not hitherto used by us.*

If, for example, the major triad is altered in this manner, there arise

a. Modulations:

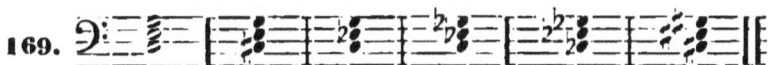

169.

Through C♯, the *diminished triad* of the seventh degree in D major or D minor, or the second degree in B minor;

Through E♭, the C minor—triad;

Through E♭ and G♭, the *diminished triad* of the seventh degree of D♭ major and minor, or the second degree of B♭ minor.

The last two alterations are mere *transpositions* of the same chord into other keys, viz., C♭ major and C♯ major.

b. *New Formations:*

170.

Of these, the formations *a, b, d, f,* can indeed be produced accident ally through *by-tones* (passing tones); they have, however, no harmonic value.

It is otherwise with the formations at *c* and *e,* which maintain harmonic (accordliche) significance.

The first form of the triad (*c*) is known under the name of

THE AUGMENTED TRIAD.

This chord was found before upon the third degree in minor (see page 13); it appears seldom, however, in this situation, as has been previously mentioned, but more often as *triad* of the *first, fourth* and fifth degrees in major, with chromatically raised fifth.

Its origin from the passing tone (G♯) to the next following (A) is easy of explanation, as also its progression, which is determined through this tone (G♯) as augmented interval.

The inversions of this chord can also be used.

Although these chords appeared for the most part in passing, or through preparation of the augmented fourth, they can also enter free in case of a rapid change of the harmony:

To the augmented triad can be added not only the *dominant seventh,* which occurs most frequently, but also the *major seventh* of the first and fourth degrees.

a.   *The augmented triad in connection with the dominant seventh:*

b. *In connection with the seventh of the first degree:*

c. *The addition of the seventh to the augmented triad of the fourth degree is very rare:*

In all these chord-connections thus far, the cadencing Bass progression, (*e. g.*, V–I I–IV) has been used: some examples, however, may show, that these chords treated of can also be used with chords of other degrees, and a various progression of the Bass.

These occasionally strange and rough sounding harmonic combinations acquire significance only *through the situation* which they occupy, and especially, if in a certain degree an *inner* necessity leads to them.

If it is the province of a text-book to call attention to the possibility of such harmonic formations, it is also its duty to warn the beginner against over valuing the *worth* of such stimulants; to advise him in general, *not*

*to occupy himself with such things and speculations, until he is fully
versed in the treatment of the simplest harmonies of the simple pure
harmonic structure.* A too early occupation therewith, and intentional
seeking out of especial effects will render difficult, and probably impossible
the clear view, and the insight into the simple, fundamental features of
harmony, and turn away the sense from the chief thing to secondary
matters.

Exercises.

REMARK.—In the fourth exercise the augmented fifth has been used, even with the
minor triad of the second degree (at NB), which in this connection does not sound unnatural. This would correspond to the formation *f* before in Example No. 170. It
is seen from this, that with a natural leading of the voices, many new chord-formations
can be gained.

From the formation *e* of example 170: (which also occurs

under the name, *double diminished triad*), arises a harmony which is much
used, viz:

THE AUGMENTED CHORD OF THE SIXTH.

The first inversion of the above chord gives it:

According to its progression, which is determined by the *augmented
sixth*, the original chord belongs here to G minor, the fourth degree of
which, C minor, with a raising of the fundamental, goes to the fifth degree

Wherever this chord appears with its natural progression shown above,

Example No. 179, the *last chord* shows itself as *dominant* The proof of this lies in a few harmonies formed like the augmented chord of the sixth, the *augmented chord of the sixth, fourth and third*, and the *augmented chord of the sixth and fifth*, the explanation of the basis of which follows farther on.

REMARK.—The relation, in which the augmented chord of the sixth stands to the just noticed chords, allows its origin to be referred to the same source. See later.

The *augmented chord of the sixth* has the peculiarity, that *its third only* (the fifth of the original chord) can be doubled in the four-voiced movement :

180.

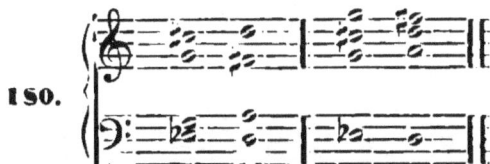

Of the remaining positions of the original chord (the so-called **double diminished** triad), the *first* (fundamental position) can be used three-voiced, but very seldom, the *third* (second inversion), also four-voiced, only however, in a very open position.

181.

REMARK.—The chromatic alteration of an interval of the minor triad is already contained in the formations of Nos. 169 and 170, and thus needs no farther investigation. Just so the chromatic alteration of an interval of the diminished triad will either produce major, or minor triads, or formations which are already found above in the place referred to.

Thus the formation of the triad in No. 170, *d* will be like the following, which is found in C major :

182.

This chord bears, in many text-books, the name : *harsh diminished triad*, *hart vonminderter Dreiklang).*

The like chords, if they may be so called, appear generally only accidentally, in *passing*, and their progression proceeds in accordance with their intervals. that is, *augmented* intervals progress one degree *upwards, diminished* intervals *downwards.*

The *chromatic alteration* of an interval of the *chord of the seventh* has been, in part, already mentioned, where to the chromatically altered triad the seventh was also added (page 92). This occurred with the augmented triad.

Among the remaining *secondary chords of the seventh*, the chromatic alteration of *one* receives an especial importance. This is *the chord of the seventh of the second degree in minor*, which, in the following form produces chord-formations much used.

The chromatic raising of its *third*

183.

gives the following inversions :

184.

Of these inversions, the *second* is the most important and is much used, the rest are unusual.

The chord resulting from the second inversion is known under the name of

THE AUGMENTED CHORD OF THE SIXTH, FOURTH AND THIRD.

Its progression is based upon that of the fundamental chord, that is, as the chord of the seventh of the second degree leads most immediately to the *dominant,* so also will this.

185.

If the fundamental of this chord is omitted, the *augmented chord of the sixth,* already found, arises, the progression of which to the dominant is hereby explained, (see page 94) ;

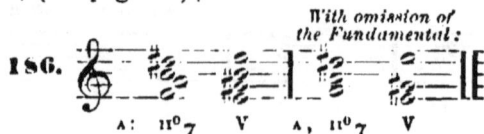

186.

With omission of the Fundamental:

or, for comparisor with No. 179, in G minor :

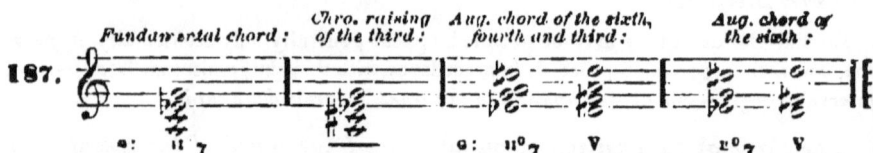

Fundamental chord :   *Chro. raising of the third :*   *Aug. chord of the sixth, fourth and third :*   *Aug. chord of the sixth :*

187.

REMARK It may be mentioned here, that the formation of the augmented chord of the sixth, fourth and third can be already reached through the *harsh diminished triad* (*hart verminderter Dreiklang*) mentioned page 95, to which a seventh is added; that the resolution, however, must become a different one, since that was considered to be on the *seventh degree*, while this is found upon the *second*.

Instead of the fundamental of this chord, the *ninth* of the fundamental chord can be added, whereby the

AUGMENTED CHORD OF THE SIXTH AND FIFTH
arises.

Its origin is as follows :

Of these chords, the one resulting from the first inversion *a*, the *augmented chord of the sixth and fifth*, is best adapted for use, the others are rare.

Its natural progression is likewise to the dominant, but always produces *parallel fifths :*

These progressing fifths, which do not belong to the most unpleasant ones, are avoided either through an *earlier* resolution of the fifth (the original, above-mentioned ninth as suspension), as in the following Example (*a*), or through a skip of the same into the third, whereby the augmented chord of the sixth results (*b*), or most frequently, by the third and fifth remaining stationary while the sixth and the Bass tone progress, whereby the chord of the sixth and fourth is inserted before the resolution (*c*), which chord can be here regarded as a prolongation of the suspension.

REMARK.—The addition of the ninth does not justify explaining this harmony as a chord of the ninth; the ninth has here, as everywhere, the same character as suspension, as appears very plainly from the progression *a ;* just so the progression at *b* are c answ... completely to the treatment of the suspensions. as it also (as fifth in the above chord) requires a preparation.

It would follow from this, that this harmony should be taken into consideration first in connection with the suspensions, it was however necessary to mention it here, because the question of the origin was under discussion. and it was not the intention, by the above expressed view, to oppose a generally received *appellation*.

Exercises.

At the close of this chapter we survey once more the broad field which was opened in it for harmonic formations. We have found much which is generally known and adapted for use. Much appeared to us unadapted for use and worthless. Nothing however showed itself in its original condition, everything had received an addition, experienced an alteration, in a certain sense, adornment. This forsaking of the *original* gives us occasion to refer once more to that which was remarked on page 93.

A long time indeed elapsed, before these harmonic transformations were discovered, and a still longer, before they became common property: much, which until now is unadapted for use, may with time be developed, but, in order that the healthy inner germ may not be lost, we cannot advise the direction of the whole effort, out of desire for originality, to the discovery of new harmonic forms, or the immoderate use of them, and deviation from the primitive.

Since all these transformations serve more for adornment, and it might be said, for the more elegant carrying out of the simple fundamental idea, we may venture to use them only with discrimination if we do not wish to overload the work of art, and thereby ourselves be reckoned as without taste.

At the close of the exhibition of all essential harmonies and their most immediate use, may still follow a brief *view* of them, their *varieties* and *derivatives*.

View of all Chords belonging to a Major or Minor Key.

I. FUNDAMENTAL HARMONIES.

a. The Triad.

b. The chord of the seventh.

A. *The varieties of the Triad:*

Major, Minor, Diminished, Augmented.

Major Triads.

Of the Major Scale:

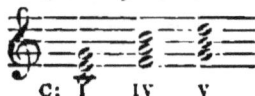

Of the Minor Scale:

C: I   IV   V

A: V   VI

Minor Triads.

Of the Major Scale:

Of the Minor Scale:

C: II   III   VI

A: I   IV

Diminished Triads.

Of the Major Scale:

Of the Minor Scale:

C: VII°

A: II°   VII°

Augmented Triad of the Minor Scale.

A: III'

B —The remaining augmented triads see under II.: *Altered Chords.*

Inversions (Versetzungen) of the Triads·

a. The chord of the sixth.

b. The chord of the sixth and fourth.

6

6
4

B   *The Varieties of the Chord of the Seventh.*

a.   *The dominant chord of the seventh or primary chord of the seventh*

b.   *Secondary chords of the seventh.*

a.   *Dominant chord of the seventh* (major triad with minor seventh).

Formed alike in Major and Minor:

C: V$_7$ c: V$_7$ A: V$_7$

b.   *Secondary chords of the seventh*

1. *Major triad with major seventh*

In Major.   *In Minor.*

C: I$_7$ IV$_7$ A: VI$_7$

2. *Minor triad with minor seventh*

In Major.   *In Minor.*

C: II$_7$ III$_7$ VI$_7$ A: IV$_7$

3. *Diminished triad with minor seventh*

In Major: *In Minor:*

C: VII^c$_7$ A: II^0$_7$

4. *Diminished triad with diminished seventh* (chord of the diminished seventh)

In Minor:

A: VII^0$_7$

5. *Augmented triad with major seventh*

In Minor:

A: III'$_7$

Inversions (Versetzungen) *of the Chords of the Seventh.*

a. The chord of   *b.* The chord of the   *c.* The chord of
the sixth and fifth :   sixth, fourth and third :   the second :

II. ALTERED (CHROMATICALLY CHANGED) CHORDS.

a. *The augmented triad*, formed from the major triad :

In Major :

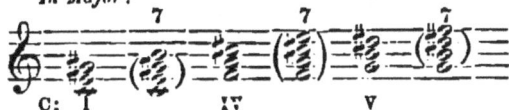

b. *The augmented chord of the sixth*, formed

1. From the minor triad with raised fundamental (so-called **double diminished triad**) :

2. From the chord of the seventh of the second degree in minor. (**See** the following chords) :

c. *The augmented chord of the sixth, fourth and third ;*

d. *The augmented chord of the sixth and fifth,*—both formed from the chord of the seventh of the second degree in minor :

Raising of the third :	*Second Inversion :*	*Without Fundamental, aug. chord of the sixth :*	*With the ninth from the Fundamental and without the latter.*

CHAPTER XI.

On Modulation of a Passage of Music (eines Tonsatzes).

THE term *modulation* has a various signification. Formerly was under stood thereby the way and manner in which the succession of harmonies is arranged to a vocal part. In the later sense is understood the *digression from one key into another*. The name, *digressive modulation*, which is sometimes found, would be no pleonasm according to the original signification of the word.

According to the import of the term, it will next be important, to learn rightly to recognize and determine each occurring modulation (digression into a foreign key); farther on, in Chapter XVI., the *means* for modulation will be discussed, whereby the capability of recognizing the latter is more fully supplied.

A modulation arises, if a harmony FOREIGN *to the previous key appears.*

The previous key is then wholly forsaken, and the harmonies must be reckoned to the new key, so long as no harmony, again foreign to it, appears which effects a new modulation.

Thus in the following Example:

192.

is a modulation to D minor in the third measure, because C♯–E–G–B♭, belongs no longer to C major, but undeniably to D minor, whereas in the fourth measure it is doubtful whether the C triad, which is foreign to the previous key (D minor), is to be reckoned to C major, or to the G major following, while the modulation to A minor in the fifth measure is unmistakable.

The dominant chord of the seventh, as also the *chord of the diminished seventh*, are, as the chief means of modulation, never to be mistaken; all the remaining chords are *ambiguous*, that is, they can belong to several keys.

Thus the G major triad belongs not exclusively to G major, but is also sub-dominant to D major and sixth degree to B minor.

This ambiguity often allows the modulation to be recognized first from the succeeding chords, as in fact, the decided modulation itself can be formed first through the *dominant harmony of the seventh* with its derivatives.

The musical ear itself proceeds very simply in the apprehension of a modulation: it always apprehends the foreign harmony as belonging to that key, which is nearest related to the ruling one.

Thus, for example, in

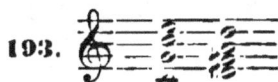

the major triad of D in itself considered, would belong to the key of D major; in connection, however, with C major, it will be most immediately recognized as dominant to G major, and the following chords first can determine which key becomes the ruling one.

There follow here some more exercises for practice in searching out the modulations; for the farther discussion of this subject see Chapter XVI

Exercises.

The modulation can be indicated in the same manner as in the first exercises, according to which the letters indicate the key and the Roman numbers, as we know, the degrees upon which the chords in question rest.

PART II.

ACCIDENTAL CHORD-FORMATIONS.—TONES FOREIGN TO THE HARMONY.

CHAPTER XII.

Suspensions.

THE *simultaneous* progression of all voices to the following chord, par ticularly if, as in our previous examples, it takes place through no *metrical* variety of the movement, produces a certain measured character and monotony of the musical sentences.

A new chaining together and binding of the chords, and a thereby more interesting change of harmonic connections arises, if the voices do not everywhere progress simultaneously; if one or several of them linger in their places, while others already form the component parts of the next harmony.

The most important manner of thus linking harmonies together, and the one to be preferred is the

SUSPENSION.

This arises through the delaying of a progression of a voice, which is expected at a definite time, or even necessary, and in such a manner, that the voice, which has to progress one degree *downwards*, in order to occupy its position in the following chord, lingers still upon the tone of the *first* chord, while the others progress to the *second*, and this voice does not pass over into the harmony until *later*.

In the following connection of harmony:

195.

the Soprano can linger upon the C during the entrance of the second chord, and pass over later to the B in the following manner :

196.

Just so a suspension can be formed from Example No. 195, through the delaying of the Tenor :

197.

That which is characteristic of the suspensions is, that they *form a dissonance* against the harmony with which they appear, and that they thereby act as a means for harmonic connection, since they render the necessary relations of two chords more intimate through the resolution expected.   In this respect they have a similarity with the *sevenths*, in common with which, as connecting intervals, they require *preparation* as well as resolution.

The dissonant character of the suspension is, to be sure, not always contained in the interval of it which disagrees harmonically with any particular voice ; cases can occur, where the suspension disagrees as interval with no one of the other voices, but where the *character* of the suspension appears only through situation, position [in the chord] and progression ; as in Example No. 197, where the tone of suspension forms a chord of the sixth and where only the unusual appearance, as well as the entire situation o. the triad of the third degree, combined with the progression of the Tenor, produces the character of the suspension.

The above examples give the rules necessary in the formation of the suspensions :

A suspension can be formed with a descending progression of a voice by degrees, under the following conditions ; it must

1. *Be prepared*, and
2. *Resolve itself*.

There will, therefore, be *three* things to observe in connection with the suspension : its *preparation* *the suspension itself* and its *position*, and *its resolution* (progression).

a. *The Preparation.*

The *preparation* of a suspension can take place through *either component part of a triad.* The sevenths also are used for preparation
although more rarely ; most often the *dominant seventh.*

The *preparation* takes place upon the *arsis,* the *suspension* itself
enters at the *thesis.* Besides this, the rule mentioned before (page 71) applies, viz., that the preparation may be of a duration *equal with* or *longer*
than the suspension, but not shorter.

b. *The Suspension.*

The *entrance of the suspension* at the thesis has just been mentioned,
its position in other respects should be still more particularly explained.

The suspension can appear in any voice, before an interval of th
triad,—before the seventh, only in rare cases.

Concerning the suspensions in case of the fifth, reference may be made to that which was remarked in connection with Example No. 197. Thus the first and third examples will be entirely in the character of the suspension, while the fourth is not to be called a suspension at all. If a seventh is added to the chord, as in the second example, the dissonant character of the suspension immediately shows itself.

That the seventh can but seldom have a suspension, appears from the fact, that it [the suspension] would necessarily be formed in most cases by the perfect octave, which in and for itself is only an interval of reduplication, and can never come into a dissonant position (*a*), except as in the following Example *b*, where the octave is *diminished.*

In the first case the seventh will always be a *passing* one.

c. *The Resolution.*

The resolution of the suspension ensues, as was remarked before, *in the same voice, by a step downwards.*

REMARK.—Ways of resolution which deviate from this will be shown later.

Here it is further to be observed that

The *tone of resolution* (the tone which is delayed by a suspension) *can be contained in no other voice; only the Bass or the lowest voice can receive it without disadvantage to the harmony.*

201.

In Example *a* the Tenor steps from A to C, which last, in the *Soprano*, is suspended by D; in Example *c* the Tenor receives the G, which, in the Alto, has the suspension A. Both reduplications are faulty, especially because they concern the *third* and *fifth* of the chord. In Example *d* at NB., the reduplication takes place with the *fundamental*. In this case the effect is better, especially if the consistency of the leading of the voices necessitates it as in the following movement:

202.

REMARK.—It may still be remarked here, that the doubling of the fundamental always assumes the distance of at least an *octave*, and that the doubling in *unison* is faulty, *e. g*

The suspension can indeed appear in such proximity, only between Bass and Tenor, or with the voice which lies next to the lowest.

The lowest voice, commonly the Bass, has, however, as the one which determines the chord, the power of counterweight against the dissonance of the suspension; reduplications are therefore admissible, if they are based upon a good leading of the voices, *e. g.*

The faulty progression of the Soprano and Bass in the last example becomes clear, if the suspension as mere delay of the progression of the voice, is taken away, through which means the *open octaves* appear:

The relation is the same with the fifth-successions, which are covered through the suspension:

Here, however, the considerations will rule, which are to be had in view in the case of the *covered fifths* in general, since position, situation, progression can permit such leading of the voices, without the unpleasantness of the fifths appearing.

We condense these remarks into the following rule:

The suspension does not remove parallel octaves and fifths; the following progression will, therefore, be faulty:

Parallel fifths of this kind are not, however, to be unconditionally rejected if through the movement of the other voices a compensation is made for the unpleasant succession, so that they do not appear too plainly. To give positive directions regarding them is impossible; to reject them always would confine us too much

The *suspensions in the Bass*, which occur oftenest *before the third* of the chord (or, which is the same thing, before the chords of the sixth and of the sixth and fifth), allow of *no reduplication in the other voices.*

207.

The suspensions before the fundamental and the fifth rarely show themselves practicable.

208.

The indication of the suspensions in the Thorough-Bass notation is, in part, contained in the previous examples.

If the suspension lies in one of the three upper voices, its interval from the Bass is given at the same time with the resolution, e. g., $\frac{5}{4}$ $\overline{3}$, 9 8, 7 6, the remaining figures determine the chord where it becomes necessary, e. g., the chord of the sixth $\frac{9}{6}$ $\frac{8}{\_}$, the chord of the sixth and fourth $\frac{6}{5}$ $\overline{\frac{}{4}}$ or $\frac{7}{4}$ $\frac{6}{\_}$.

If the suspension lies in the lower voice, the chance intervals of the remaining voices are likewise indicated by numbers, e. g., $\frac{5}{2}\overline{\_}$, or in case of the chord of the seventh $\frac{o}{4}\overline{\_}$; the dashes which follow denote that the voices retain their tones during the resolution of the suspension.

The suspension in the Bass is also marked by a diagonal stroke above it and the corresponding chord set over the tone of resolution, which plainer as concerns the latter, e. g.

209.

In the succeeding examples the first manner is chosen, as the most common.

Exercises.

It will be to the purpose in the working out of these and the succeeding exercises, to separate the voices and write each upon an especial staff. This notation, in the manner of a score, affords a better view of the course of each particular voice, and is in general a useful preparatory exercise in score reading.

Here, however, it becomes necessary to write the voices, which, in the pure harmonic structure, must always be conceived of as voices to be sung, in the clefs which have always been allotted to them, the knowledge of which is indispensable to every musician. The knowledge of these clefs can be very soon attained by attentive practice, and through comparison with those already known.

REMARK.—The knowledge of the Alto and Tenor clefs is requisite for the understanding and reading of scores, since many voices and instruments are exclusively or partially written in these clefs, and the Soprano clef itself, which occurs more rarely, affords with various instruments, which are tuned in a particular way, an especial facility in reading.

The clef which is used for the upper three voices, Soprano, Alto, and Tenor, is called the *C-clef.*

For the lowest vocal part, the Bass, the F-clef or Bass clef used before is still applied.

The situation of the C-clef always indicates the place of the *once marked* [middle] C, and in such a manner, that for the *Soprano* this C is found upon the *lowest*, for the *Alto* upon the *third*, and for the *Tenor* upon the *fourth line, e. g.*

The most common compass of the voices exhibits itself in these clefs thus ·

REMARK.—The origin of these various clefs from the most simple foundation, from the so-called Tablature (commonly a system of ten lines, upon which all the voices were written, with especial designation of the lines upon which the principal tones, F, C, G, came to stand) is interesting, its farther explanation would here, however, lead us too far.

The easiest method of impressing these clefs upon the memory, is probably, to observe accurately the position of the C-triad in the various voices, whereby the tones which lie between and on each side are easily found out.

Thus the position of the complete C-triad, with doubling of the fundamental, will be :

In the Soprano:

In the Alto :

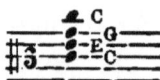

In the Tenor, best in the position of the chord of the sixth and fourth :

The carrying out of the first exercise of No. 210 in these clefs follows here :

211.

SOPRANO.

ALTO.

TENOR.

BASS.

C: I   V   IV   V$\frac{7}{7}$ I   II$\frac{7}{7}$ V$\frac{7}{7}$ I

The working out of these examples requires, with all observance of the rules thus far given, a skillful and a freer leading of the voices in relation to their position, since the necessity of a better position of the suspension often renders necessary even an alteration of the position of the voices, which we have hitherto always endeavored to make as uniform as possible.

In this manner the *open* position of the voices will come, of itself, and again be necessarily exchanged for the *close* position where necessity and conformity with the end in view require it.

In this exchange of the position of the voices, the following rules must be observed :

The voices can never, SIMULTANEOUSLY, move by degrees or skip out of their necessary position from one chord to another (foreign one), except in individual cases in the transposition of ONE and THE SAME chord into other positions.

Any voice can forsake its position, if one or more remain stationary upon one tone.

The following carrying out of Exercise 8 of No. 210, will make this plainer

The following may serve as explanation of this treatment.

The close position in which this example begins, is forsaken in the fifth measure, in which the open begins, and remains until in the eleventh measure the close position again appears.

This was effected through a freer leading of the Soprano and Tenor
The first makes a skip, in the fifth measure, out of its position into the
seventh E♭ (at NB.), a skip which can take place if the *fundamental* is
already present and remains stationary (as here the F in the Bass); in
like manner it forsakes the position in the seventh measure, by a skip into
the fifth, G, *the chord remaining stationary*, whereby the suspension comes
into a better position. At last the close position is attained again through
the better and free leading of the Tenor in the tenth measure.

Suspensions from Below Upward.

Suspensions from below are only in a few isolated cases to be regarded
as such; most progressions of this kind arise out of the suspensions from
above, before treated of, through *contraction* (abbreviation) of the same
with a farther succession in a upward direction, *e. g.*

The suspension from below can take place in connection with the pro
gression of the *leading tone* :

also with several intervals, which progress a half-step upwards, especially
with those altered chords, which receive augmented intervals through
elevation, *e. g.*

Observe here, that as before, the tone of resolution (harmonic tone)
must be in *no other voice* with the exception of the Bass.

REMARK.—The last of the above examples brings us the same tone-combination
which presented itself before (page 64) as chord of the seventh of the first degree in
minor, and which was explained as unfit for use as fundamental harmony. (See page
74). That, in the above application, it is to be considered as suspension of the leading
tone, requires no farther explanation.

Of other suspensions, especially those which progress a *whole* step upwards:

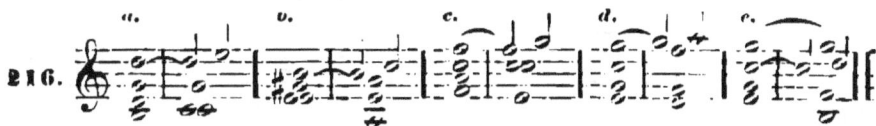

some show, of themselves, the unnaturalness of their progression; and some the theory must pronounce not genuine, and unfit for use for the pure harmonic structure, however often they may find place in the practice. If these false suspensions should be carried out after the manner previously shown (No. 213), faulty progressions would show themselves, upon which they are based:

Suspensions in more than one Voice.

Suspensions can occur in more than one voice at the same time ·

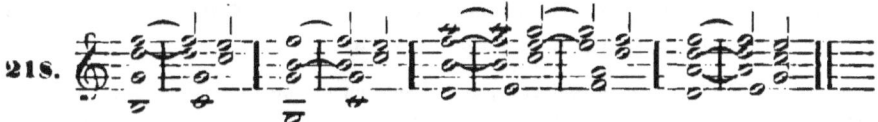

The chord of the sixth and fourth frequently shows itself as **double** suspension, *e. g.*

Freer Movement of the Voices in the Resolution of the Suspensions.

Preparation, entrance, and resolution of the suspension took place in the previous examples by means of *two* chords, since the voices which did not take part in it remained stationary during its resolution. The same can also take place with *three* chords, whereby the interchange of chords and the leading of the voices becomes still richer and more manifold.

This takes place, if, during the resolution of the suspension, several of the remaining voices, or one, usually the Bass, progress at the same time and by this means form a new harmony

For example, by progression of the Bass:

220.

By progression of more than one voice:

221.

In all these examples the resolution of the suspension ensues regularly during the progression of the remaining voices to a new harmony, of which the resolution-tone is, itself, a component part.

REMARK.—It may here be remarked, in explanation of the view concerning chords of the ninth expressed in Chapter IX, that many places in which the ninth occurs, and which are recognized by many as chords of the ninth, can be explained in the above manner; as in Example 221 *b,* where the cadencing Bass progression F–B could be easily explained as the progression of a secondary chord of the seventh and ninth, if the above explanation of a *suspension of a ninth with the use of three chords* were not much more simple and did not lead to the same result, and, as with all subsequent examples, present itself in the same manner:

Suspension of a ninth
with two chords: with three chords: better:

222.

Concerning the ninth which enters free, we will speak later in connection with the Organ-point.

It may still be added as completion of what was said in Chapter IX, that as a reason against independent chords of the ninth, the impossibility may apply, of bringing them into such inversion *with the fundamental* that the latter is brought into immediate proximity with the ninth, as can always take place with the chords of the seventh, *e. g*

223.

In tne same manner *four* chords can be applied with the suspension, if ꞇ stands before a harmonic tone, which is not contained in the remaining voices, *e. g.*

221.

Exercises.

225.

Between suspension and resolution, other tones can be inserted in the same voice.

These can be:

1. Tones which belong to the chord, *e. g.*

2. Tones foreign to the harmony, changing notes, *e. g.*

The explanation of these and similar instances is completed through the exhibition of the passing and changing notes found farther on.

Instances also occur, in which the suspension receives no resolution at all, *e. g.*

They have arisen from the following passages, by omission:

229.

Anticipation. (*Vorausnahme.*)

The anticipation of a tone, which is more rarely used than the suspension, is the opposite of the latter, and consists in this, that one or more voices allow some tones of the next following chord to be heard *earlier* than others, and before the *metrical division* allows us to expect them.

With notes of long duration, and in a slow movement, this manner of leading the voices occurs seldom or not at all, since the harshness of the dissonances which appear here would amount to unintelligibleness; it is mostly shorter parts of measures which are anticipated, e. g.

230.

Anticipation in the Bass: *In the Soprano:*   *In several voices:*

The similarity of this movement of the voices in its metrical form, **with** that which general musical instruction comprehends under the name *syncopated notes*, is not to be mistaken; the latter, however, are formed not by *anticipation* of the chords, but by *after-striking* (Nachschlagen) of them, or they have merely rythmical significance.

The movement of the voices can here also be freer under some circumstances; for example, a harmonic tone can be anticipated, other than that which is intended at the entrance of the chord, as in the known closing formula:

231.

As antithesis to *anticipation* may yet be adduced the *after-striking* of harmonic tones, which has a similarity with the suspensions, in so far, as also here preparation and resolution take place, but differs again, materially as its character expresses itself more in the metrical and rythmical movement, for which reason it also always appears in more extended successions; the suspensions, however, appear under entirely other conditions, singly or in greater numbers.

The following Bass would be a succession of such after-struck tones:

Here would also belong that unison passage from the overture to 'Leonore" (No. 3) of Beethoven:

CHAPTER XIII.

The Organ Point. Stationary Voices.

An especial manifold character of the harmonies, and a mingling of them, arises by means of one or even more than one of the voices remaining stationary upon one tone, and by means of the chords thereby accidentally formed.

We frequently meet (particularly in the Bass) as well at the beginning of a composition, as in the middle and at the conclusion, at the point where the cadence should begin, with a long sustained tone, during the continuance of which the remaining voices, apparently without reference to it, continue their harmonic movement.

If this tone lies in the Bass, it is called

ORGAN-POINT [Pedal Point];

f such prolonged tones occur in the other voices, the latter are called

STATIONARY VOICES or STATIONARY TONES.

REMARK.—Many give these last also the name Organ-Point, but incorrectly.

The tones, which are adapted for remaining stationary are the *tonic* and *dominant;* they also occur *together.*

REMARK.—Attempts with the third of the triad, which in later times have been instituted by many composers, betray too plainly to the ear the unnatural and far sought.

The harmonic connection, as well as the progression of the remaining voices takes place, always, during the organ-point, according to the known rules, so that the next lower voice assumes the conduct of the harmony, and in general without regard to the stationary tone.

Before we enter more particularly into the manner of treating the organ-point, some examples may follow

a.   *Organpoint* upon the tonic:

231.

b. Upon the dominant:

c. or:

d. Upon both at the same time:

In these examples, those chords to which the Bass tone does not harmonically belong, are marked by a cross.

The following remarks may serve for the treatment of the organ-point:

1. *The entrance of the organ-point takes place at a rythmically definite time;*

2. *By means of a chord to which the Bass tone harmonically belongs;*

3. *The last chord of the organ-point must likewise be in harmony with it.*

The first takes place at the beginning or close of a period or division of one and upon the *thesis;* the second and third commonly by means of the fundamental of a triad, as in Example No. 234 *a, c, d,* or at *b,* through the chord of the sixth and fourth.

Care should be taken, further, that the chords *foreign* to the Bass tone do not succeed each other too frequently, but are often interchanged with chords to which the organ-point harmonically belongs. This is necessary in order to avoid digressions violating the character of the organ-point which is only to be found in the holding firmly together of various chord combinations.

Thus the following organ-point would be faulty in this regard .

235.

The voice lying next to the Bass, in a four-voiced movement, the Tenor, becomes, in case of the organ-point, the fundamental voice of the harmonic leading. Therefore, all necessary harmonic progressions will be conditioned by this voice, even if the organ-point should also, accidentally, belong to the harmony. Thus, in Example No. 234 *a*, the progression of the B♭ in the Alto (in the first measure) is determined by the leading of the remaining voices, and not by the circumstance that it is seventh to the Bass.

If the organ-point stands upon the dominant, as is often the case at the close, no plagal close can be formed upon it, as appears already from the third of the above adduced rules, *e. g.*

236.

The plagal close can, however, ensue with the organ-point of the tonic:

237.

The end of the organ-point is indeed to be just as carefully treated as its entrance. In the examples brought forward above, this always takes place through a cadence. In this case it presents no difficulty, except in instances such as at No. 236. The organ-point can, however, also pass over earlier to the harmonic leading, and then the third rule is to be carefully observed, *e. g.*

228.

Breaking off in the following manner would not, however, be good:

239.

Stationary Voices.

Upper or middle voices remaining stationary upon one tone, in the manner of the organ-point before described, are much more rare than the latter, and require greater caution in their treatment.

Sustained tones of this kind only conform to the character of these voices if chords not belonging to them appear *very rarely* in connection with them, since such voices do not possess the power of counterweight against foreign chords, which is peculiar to the Bass or the lower voice as the determining one.

Thus the organ-point of Example No. 234 *a*, being transposed into the upper voice, will in the last measures, sound very unpleasant:

240.

while the following tone, prolonged as dominant, is better because the last chords of the example belong to it:

241.

As example of effective use of stationary voices and prolonged tones and for their treatment, a place can be adduced in the "Gloria" of Cherubini's Mass in C-major, where the violins hold A♭ for a length of time while the choir and instruments taking part, carry out below it their particular melodic and harmonic progressions; just so the D of the violins in the introduction to the overture "Meeresstille und glückliche Fahrt" of Mendelssohn Bartholdy. In both cases but few chords can be found to which the prolonged tone would not be harmonic.

Under this head may also be reckoned the Trio of the Scherzo of Beethoven's Symphony in A-major, which is based throughout upon the A which shows itself sometimes as stationary tone in the upper and middle voices, sometimes as organ-point in the lowest voice, and serves throughout the whole piece as basis.

Stationary tones in the middle voices are to be treated with the same care, as those in the upper voice. In instrumental compositions they always appear strengthened according to the circumstances; in the four voiced movement they occur rarely and not in too great length, e. g.

242.

REMARK.—As completion of what was said of the chords of the ninth, the following may here still find place:

In the foregoing Example *b*, if the stationary voice be included [in the reckoning], a complete chord of the ninth is found in an inverted position with regular resolution. It has already been remarked in objection to the chords of the ninth, that their inversions cannot be so used that fundamental and ninth are brought into immediate proximity, as in the case of the sevenths. That they can occur together at greater distances, as above, furnishes no ground for regarding them as independent chords, since they occur only in the relations there found, viz., in connection with a stationary tone the character of which is, however, also to bear harmonies foreign to it, as, for example, is the case with the following ninth, which certainly forms no chord of the ninth.

243.

If we wish to mark by numbers the harmonic progression above the
organ-point, they must always have reference to the stationary tone in the
Bass, whereby in many cases the otherwise general marking of the chords
is altered.

Thus the organ-point found under No. 234 *b*, could be marked thus ·

Such a manner of marking is only used for especial purposes, on account of the difficulty of reading it and also its incompleteness, for which
reason, in scores where a figuring is introduced, we often find with the
organ-point the words *tasto solo*, which indicates that, with the otherwise
customary organ accompaniment, only the organ-point itself is to be given.

CHAPTER XIV.

Passing Notes.   Changing Notes.

AMONG the tones foreign to the harmony are especially to be reckoned
the *passing* and *changing* notes.

The first arise through the filling out, by means of tones lying between,
of greater or smaller harmonic voice-steps, *e. g.*

The notes marked by a cross × form the *pass*, those marked with a o
are *harmonic by-tones*, that is, in so far as with the first note a C or
A-triad can be conceived, *e. g.*

246.

The passing notes found under *a* of Example No. 245 are called **dia-**
tonic, those under *b* *chromatic* passes.

The passing notes go from one harmonic note over to another har-
monic note; they appear, therefore, not with the entrance of the chord, but
after it, upon smaller divisions of the measure, and can be introduced
only in progression *by degrees.*

Changing notes, on the contrary, are those tones foreign to the harmony, which either appear in the *character of a suspension* or *appog-*
giatura at the time of the entrance of the harmony (thus in this sense upon
the accented part of the measure), and attach themselves to the harmonic
note (No. 247 *a*), or, after the manner of the passing notes upon the unaccented part, serve for the melodic adornment of *two like notes.* (No.
247 *b*).

247.

The changing note can therefore appear IN SKIPS, *it must however be*
joined closely to the harmonic note, as the examples in No. 247 show.

It is further to be seen from the above examples, that the changing
notes can be formed by the note which lies immediately *below* the harmonic note, as well as by the one which lies immediately *above.*

The changing note *below* the harmonic note, especially if it enter after
the manner of an appoggiatura, upon the accented part of the measure, has
the peculiarity that it inclines to form a *minor second* to the principal
note, whereby chromatic tones arise, as is to be seen from No. 247, hence
the formation of movements like the following would not be admissible:

This applies particularly to the changing notes introduced by skips.

It is otherwise if they appear in a progressing series, whereby they take on the character of the passing notes. Thus the following series of changing notes at *a* would not, of necessity, be so formed as at *b*.

Those changing notes below, which fall upon the unaccented part, require only partially the minor second. Thus, in the Example No. 250 *a*, the formation will not necessarily be like *b*, while *c* is not so good as *d*.

Definite rules on this head cannot be given; it is also unnecessary, in a each as every musical ear will certainly find that which is right.

REMARK.—The third of the triad bears the changing note as *whole* step better than the fifth and octave. Since with the latter the changing note can appear at the same time as seventh, so that the *succession* only can determine in respect to it.

Changing notes *above* the harmonic note, whether they enter free (by skips), or in the manner of No. 250, can form *major* or *minor seconds* to the chord-tone because they are always formed diatonically, and govern themselves according to the key and modulation.

We often meet with figures, in which changing notes above and below the chord note are made use of one after the other, *e. g.*

Upon this is founded also the following often occurring manner of embellishment:

253.

Passing and changing notes can occur in all voices. If this takes place, by preference, in *one* voice alone, this one will become prominent in comparison with the others, and receive a concerting character, while the remaining voices serve for accompaniment. If this should not be the case, all the voices can be made prominent, interchangeably, by such by-tones, and gain thereby in significance. Wherever the position and progression of a voice adapts it for the introduction of such by-tones, it will by this means admit of more significant melodic development; but here also the proper mean must be found, since, otherwise, over fullness and a lack of clearness can easily arise.

The following simply harmonic movement,

254.

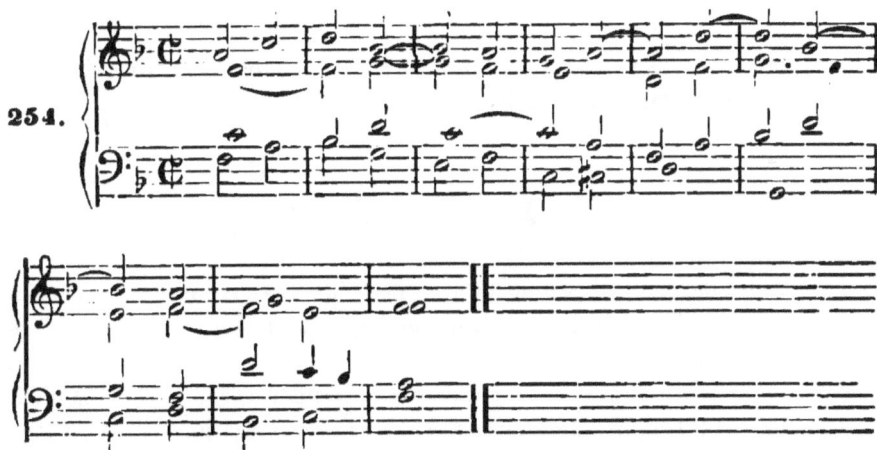

might, by the use of the above by-tones, assume the following form:

255.

The passing and changing notes are here marked by crosses ×

That through such copious use of tones foreign to the harmony, the passage can easily suffer from overloading. is to be seen in the above example if it is executed in a somewhat rapid tempo; a slow movement is better adapted to this manner of writing.

In the introduction of the changing notes, care is to be taken, as was before remarked in connection with the suspensions, *that no voice receives the harmonic tone which in another is introduced through a changing note, e. g.*

This can only occur if the distance of the harmonic tone from the tone oreign to the harmony is at least one octave, *e. g.*

This reduplication, according to the principles of reduplication in general, will take place better with the fundamental or fifth, than with the third of the fundamental chord.

In a rapid movement, however, and more extended carrying. out of such figures formed through changing notes, other considerations arise, as the following passage shows; this to be sure, cannot be conceived of as a four-voiced vocal movement:

In the case of the regular passing notes, like regard is to be had to their approximation to harmonic tones, and figures such as No. 259 *a, b,* do not appear so pure as *c, d, e.*

259.

More rapid figures allow this approximation more readily, *e. g.*

260.

Faulty Progressions in Connection with Passing and Changing Notes.

Since it is the province of the passing notes to fill out the *movement in skips* of the harmonic progression, we must take care in connection with the change of the harmony, that no false progressions arise, as in the following examples, from covered fifths *open* ones arise:

261.

Open octaves formed with *passing tones* cannot occur, because the first of them will be harmonic as much as the second.

262.

On the other hand, in the following instances, the passing notes will not cover the open octaves, and consequently will be considered as faulty ·

263.

REMARK.—The last kind of octaves would find application in *instrumental movements*, under the condition of intended strengthening and reduplication.

In like manner the entrance or progression of the *changing note* in parallel movement is to be called faulty if it takes place in the following manner ·

261.

The last example is better because the octave progression appears covered.

Passing and Changing Notes in more than one Voice at the same time.

The movement of the passing notes in more than one voice at the same time is best adapted, in parallel motion, to the successions of thirds and ixths, *e. g.*

265.

The free movement of the voices with the use of the passing notes can also produce parallel seconds, fourths, fifths, and sevenths, of all kinds, which require great caution in their treatment, and on account of their disagreeable effect are only to be allowed *singly*, and in a very favorable position.

Progressions in fourths are good if a third voice is added as third below :

266.

Single fifth-successions arising from passing notes are occasionally met with in good compositions, which, however, is no reason for recommending them as faultless. (See that which is said concerning fifth-successions page 27 and what follows).

Just so the harshness of the seventh-successions can only be alleviated through favorable position and good leading of the voices throughout; indeed, through tempo, movement, etc.

In *contrary movement* the various intervals of the passing notes often give to the passage an especial, peculiar coloring, and contribute much to the independence of the voices, but they must not appear too numerously and in too many voices at the same time.

267.

Here also it will be found, that those passing notes, which, outside of the simply harmonic structure lying at the basis, form with others, as it were, a most intimate, new (passing) harmonic leading, are more natural and milder than those whose collocation cannot be harmonically accounted for.

A judgment concerning the worth of such movements can, however, be arrived at only by taking into consideration their character and tempo.

In case of regular harmonic progressions, several voices can receive passing tones at the same time, *e. g.*

268.

In all such places everything depends upon the question, whether at the *hange of the harmony* the voices are in a position which allows them o form their progression *regularly.*

Changing notes can occur in various voices:

a. In *two* voices:

in parallel motion:

269.

in contrary motion:

270.

b. In *three* voices:

271.

c. In *four* voices ·

272.

REMARK.—The most of the above examples can also have the force of harmonic progressions with the organ-point.

It becomes evident from these examples, that also in the parallel movement of two voices in changing notes, the progression in thirds and sixths appears most natural, while the parallel seconds, fourths, fifths and sevenths always produce a very disagreeable effect. Thus no one would be likely to pronounce changing notes of the following sort, good :

good

273.

Changing notes can also be of longer duration, than the harmonic note to which they are joined, *e. g.*

274.

The significance in composition, of the subjects explained in Chapters XII., XIII. and XIV., is great enough to subject them to a careful investigation; as a thorough knowledge of them contributes materially to th understanding of the inner harmonic structure. We have still to speak concerning their relation to the pure harmonic structure—the object of our immediate studies.

Since on page 24 the term "pure harmonic structure" was only spoken of in a general way, it becomes necessary to consider the question more narrowly, and to present it something in this manner :

What application of these means for composition does our immediate purpose, (the exercises in the pure harmonic structure), allow ?

It is undeniable that these means are particularly adapted for developing and adorning the voices.

If, however, our most immediate work is the recognition and carrying out of *simple harmonic formations*, then, to be sure, everything which is adapted to *develop* the voices will be appropriately used ; but anything else, serving only for embellishment, will be excluded ; in brief, the essential must be separate from the unessential.

As belonging to the unessential will always be reckoned, firstly :

All harmonic artificialities (Künsteleien) *in general, in so far as they are founded upon no inner necessity ; unnatural introduction of little-used harmonies.* They easily produce over-fullness, swollen over-loading of the passage, and bear witness rather to a morbid or mentally weak condition, than to originality and fresh, free, powerfully secure movement ;

Then :

Irregular introduction of the suspensions ; the use of stationary voices, and of the anticipated and after-struck tones ;

Especially, however :

The changing notes which are struck free and the figures formed therefrom ; in short, everything which appears inappropriate to a simple, good four-voiced song.

If, in fact, vocal composition is received as the basis upon which all music is founded, then much in connection with it will of itself remain excluded, which is appropriate to instrumental compositions.

If also for practice in the use of the harmonies, and for the learning of a good and pure leading of the voices, the elaboration of chorals or simple movements in the manner of chorals is directly suggested as most to the purpose, this also will not exclude the use of those means in so far as they serve not merely for embellishment but for the development of the leading of the voices.

Among these is especially to be reckoned the use of the suspensions and of the regular passing and changing notes.

In accordance with the foregoing, the strictness of the pure harmonic structure in connection with the first study of harmony, and later contrapuntal labors may now be judged, which forbids many things the practice likes to use in appropriate places, as not to the purpose, immaterial, and as causing deviation from the chief object.

The thorough study of good compositions will serve for the complete understanding of all subjects thus far discussed. Chapter XIX. in Part III of this book, in which we return to this subject, will afford opportunity for attempts of our own.

CHAPTER XV.

Passing Chords.

THOSE are called passing chords, which in smaller parts of measures, after the manner of the passing notes in several voices, appear as actual chord-formations, in the entrance and treatment of which, however, a manner is sometimes found deviating from the general rules of chord-connection.

Of these, one kind has appeared already in such passing and changing notes in three voices, as take on the chord form, e. g., in Nos. 271 and 272. Just so, the most of the chords which are formed over an organ-point can in a certain sense be called passing chords

There are, however, still other phenomena of the kind, which are to be here explained.

As, in general, passing and changing notes depend principally upon the relations of measure, it becomes necessary for the explanation of the passing chords to cast a glance at the various division of measure.

It is known, that in the simple, *even varieties of measure*, the natural accent rests upon the first measural-division, while the second receives a less weight.

If now the harmonic progression be based simply upon the two measural-divisions, then the harmonies, which come upon the accented division (Thesis) will always appear as the more weighty, and must always be conceived of as the goal to which the chords of the second divison (Arsis) lead

275

in this sense, the chords of the second measural-division can be called passing chords, although in the regular movement this character of theirs does not appear so plainly.

That this has been so understood in the theory, even if seldom plainly expressed, is shown by the fact that, at their entrance, more care has ever been bestowed upon the chords upon the thesis; and in case of those upon the arsis, much has been allowed which was not conceded to the former.

The character of the passing chords appears, however, more plainly with such harmonies as are assigned to smaller divisions of the measure, as in the following examples:

276.

277.

The peculiar manner of appearance of the chord of the sixth and fourth in Example No. 276 *a* and *c,* as well as of the chord of the seventh in *c,* is only to be explained *through* the *ensuing progression (in the character of the passing notes) of all voices, by degrees, to their nearest goal--the* chord of the thesis in the following measure.

These voices can be still more easily recognized in their character as passing, if one voice is allowed to remain stationary, for example, the Bass of No. 277 *a*, or the upper voices *b*. (See above, No. 277).

The leading of the voices in No. 276 *a*, has arisen from the application of both modes.

If this condition (the progression of the voices by degrees) is fulfilled, then all chords can enter free ; they will find explanation in the principal chord which immediately succeeds them.

278.

REMARK.—In this explanation of the passing chords, the free treatment of the seventh mentioned before, finds also its justification. (See NB.)

In the simple *uneven* varieties of measure the accent likewise falls upon the first measural-division, whereas they contain *two* measural-divisions of less weight. Passing chords will show themselves in the following manner :

279.

Smaller measural-divisions can also contain passing chords, and after the above, no example is needed for it, and just as little for the compound varieties of measure.

Here also the study of good compositions will be explanatory, and lead to advancement.

For personal attempts the following remarks may still find place :

All chords designated as passing will either progress according to the known rules of the connection of harmony, or deviate from them. In the first case, which is more frequent, no farther remark is necessary ; in the last, it will depend upon a flowing melodic leading of the voices, as well in them-

selves, as also in relation to each other, whether formations of this kind are
to be called correct. It can only be remarked in general, that *the progression
of the voices by degrees will also here determine the character of the
passing chords,* and that all such passages are to be judged after taking
into account the rythm, tempo and character of the composition.

CHAPTER XVI.

On the Means for Modulation.

THE term *modulation* has already been explained in Chapter XI.
There the object was to determine each modulation correctly; now we
are to treat *of the best means* for effecting a modulation.

The art of modulation consists in finding out those harmonies which
stand in connection with two or more keys, in order, by means of these to
pass from one key into the other.

Every modulation can be effected in various ways, and will serve various
purposes. It can,

Firstly: begin abruptly, be quickly completed and pass by, or
*Secondly: be more gradually prepared for, seek out the new key as a
goai, and take it for a length of time as basis.*

In the first case it will avail itself of the simplest means, make its appearance with decision, but soon leave the new key, and perhaps, indeed
not allow it to attain to a definite development of itself; in the second case
it is commonly prepared and worked out gradually by various means, and
endeavoring to impress the new key upon the ear, will probably also lead to
a close.

Thus, in the following example:

the modulation will be transient and frequently changing, without forsaking materially the principal key, C-major.

This kind of modulation is only adapted for the nearest related keys and although more distant ones can be reached by especial and decided means, still in their development very natural and organic combinations must prevail, if they are not to appear unintelligible.

In the next example, however, the more distant key becomes the goal, which is gradually reached ; the original key is entirely forsaken, and the new one takes its place :

281.

C: I Bb: vii°7 Bb: I f: V7 Eb: V7

This example shows plainly, how the extended modulation, which sets for itself the new key as goal, makes use of the passing modulation, in order to reach it, and this the rather, as it was not the object to reach Eb major quickly.

Unless we wish to use such short passages as interlude between two compositions of different keys, or as exercises, they must be made use of in composition in a special manner, since upon the formation of the modulations themselves rests, in part, at the same time, the formation of the periods and their divisions. This, however, is an important part of the doctrine of Form, and belongs to the arrangement of the modulation of a composition, and is thus foreign to our immediate purpose.

REMARK.—An elucidation of this may be found in the author's work—"*Die Grundzüge der musikalischen Formen und ihre Analyse.*"—(Leipsic, G. Wigand.)

We make use at present of the formation of such modulations as exercises, in order thereby to promote skill in the use of the harmonics and their appropriate connection.

While the means for modulation are being searched out, no immediate attention will be paid to the *kind* of modulation used, since the same can serve for both the above designated kinds.

The first and simplest means will be

THE TONIC TRIAD OF THE NEW KEY

itself.

If, however, this triad is already a component part of the first key, then what succeeds only, and particularly the subsequent dominant harmony of the new key, will really determine the intended modulation. Thus, in the following example at *a,* no modulation will be felt, w ile at *b* we hear the key of G-major plainly only when we come to the third harmony :

282.

In case of more distant keys the *minor triad* can, to be sure, as tonic triad, have a more decided effect, still for the sake of definiteness the dominant harmony will succeed it (at *a*) ; the *major triad,* however will incline to make itself understood as dominant (*b*)

283.

As unsatisfying as the tonic triad shows itself to be, for modulation, in the way used above, in as great degree has one of its inversions (the *chord of the sixth and fourth*) the quality of rendering such modulation particularly decided. For just as it naturally takes part in the closing cadence (see pages 49 and 53), so it produces at its entrance the feeling cf a modulation, if it is not used in the manner of the passing chords, but enters at the thesis. However, in this case also, it is naturally followed by the dominant, which first completes the modulation.

284.

Upon the arsis it will not indicate the key so definitely:

285.

All examples given above, however, point to a still more potent means of modulation, viz.,

THE DOMINANT HARMONY.

The triad, as well as the chord of the seventh of the dominant, shows itself as the most natural and best means of digression, since, through it, (which applies especially to the dominant harmony of the seventh) the key is most unmistakably determined:

The modulation through the chord of the seventh of the dominant can be effected without intermediate chord in the following manner.

According to the principle that *that* connection of harmony will be most easily comprehended, which is effected through *like* or stationary tones (preparation), modulations can be effected through the dominant chord of the seventh, from the tonic major triad into all remaining keys, except the keys of the minor and major third, and that of the augmented fourth. From C-major we can reach all keys, except E♭, E and F♯, (it can remain undetermined for the present whether major or minor) thus:

286.

Everywhere in these examples the like tones, which are connected with each other by a tie, mediate the transition to the dominant of the next key; thus, from C major to D minor, the tones G and E, which become fifth and seventh of the dominant harmony, &c.

REMARK.—It only need be mentioned, that these modulations can also be reached through other positions of the chords, *e. g.*

If we wish to modulate in the same manner into the three keys which are wanting above, it can be done by means of an inserted chord (in the simplest manner, by a triad), which then supplies the missing connection *e. g.*

The modulation from the *minor* can be formed thus:

To the remaining keys C, D♭, E♭, F♯ and A♭, by means of a connecting chord :

It is self evident that this manner of modulation is only exhibited as the *simplest principle*, and that it is by no means necessary that a modulation should always take place in this way ; likewise, that as simple connections of harmony can be produced without a *stationary tone*, so also can modulations ; as, for example, the following modulations can be accomplished *without* intermediate chord :

291.

For the connection of harmonies and especially of the keys, it will, however, always be of great use to make ourselves thoroughly acquainted with this principle, and to this end to write down modulations from all keys, and therewith to bring the chords into the most various positions, as also to make these connections evident to us by performance upon the piano-forte.

This mechanical proceeding will greatly further dexterity in the use of all means of composition.

Another chord shares with the dominant chord of the seventh the capability for modulation, viz.,

THE CHORD OF THE DIMINISHED SEVENTH.

This chord, which in most cases takes the place of the dominant harmony, will frequently be more adapted for modulation than the latter, since its entrance is much milder, particularly in those cases in which seventh and fundamental of the dominant harmony would be obliged to enter free at the same time.

The following examples present the use of this chord:

292.

Beside this application, this chord shows, by means of its *enharmonic* nature, a farther, peculiar capability.

The following chords, entirely like as to sound, but variously written:

293.

belong to *four* different keys, viz.: in the first form to F minor, in the second to D minor, in the third to B minor, in the fourth to Ab minor.

Through this circumstance a fourfold modulation is possible:

294.

Since now all the chords of the diminished seventh can appear in the following three positions, as the piano-forte shows most plainly,

295.

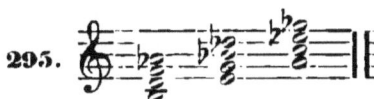

and each of them, through enharmonic interchange, will belong to *four* keys, modulations present themselves for all *twelve* keys in minor, to which in many cases we can add the twelve in major, since this chord can often be used instead of the dominant harmony in major.

Here also the industrious writing down of this manner of modulation will tend greatly to advancement in the comprehension of the inner connection of all keys, as well as of the multiplicity of harmonic connection.

Although this manner of modulation shows itself to be adapted to manifold uses in actual composition, still it must be remarked that it should not be used too often, since, being applied lightly, its artistic worth becomes less.

A similar application, though not in so comprehensive a manner, is exhibited by

THE AUGMENTED CHORD OF THE SIXTH AND FIFTH.

Its similarity as regards sound, to the dominant chord of the seventh

296.

with enharmonic change, adapts it, in connection with the latter, for modulation into certain keys, *e. g.*

297.

Although, in the above, the means were sought out with which to pass quickly from one key into the other, still (since it will not always be the intention to carry out a modulation quickly and decidedly), for the furtherance of skill the exercises can be extended and given out in the following manner:

From one key into the other by means of the triads of various degrees.

From C to D through the triad of the third degree:

298.

From C to D through the triad

Of the fourth degree: *Of the fifth degree:*   *Of the sixth degree*

299.

Of the seventh degree

From C major to E through the triad

Of the second degree: *Of the fourth degree:*   *Of the fifth degree.*

300.

Of the sixth degree: *Of the seventh degree:*

These indications may suffice for learning to form other modulations according to the same principles.

Extension of Modulation and its Completion through the Cadence.

The process shown above, for passing from one key into the other, was based upon the simplest and most natural means.

If we wish to carry out more at length a digression into a new key, the above means must, to be sure, serve to this end, they are not however applied so suddenly and directly, but the before mentioned passing modulation is used, and the new key introduced only gradually. The use of the cadence-formulæ will, however, establish the ultimate key in the best manner.

To this end we can form for ourselves the following kind of problems. *e. g.*

Let a modulation be made from C major through D minor, A minor, and G major to E minor.

This problem would be solved something in this manner:

301.

C: I   D: VII°$_7$ A: VII°$_7$ G: V$_7$ E: V$_7$

In connection with the addition of the cadence, the following is to be observed :

If the modulation takes place through the chord of the sixth and fourth of the tonic triad of the new key (see page 143), then the succession of the dominant chord with its natural progression will be sufficient for effecting the cadence, *e. g.*

In other cases the *extended cadence*, or the known closing formulæ will be requisite (see page 40) in order to determine the final key. As the simplest of such closing formulæ the following are commonly used :

If these cadence-formulæ be added to the modulation itself, according to the position of the last chord, then it is completed.

This may be shown in connection with some former examples.

The modulation from C to E♭, No. 288, closes with the fifth in the Soprano. To this is added the cadence in the position which answers to this last chord, *e. g.*

304.

The following modulation from C to ʌ in No. 286, would require a cadence in this position:

305.

The modulation from C to B with use of the cadence under No. 303 *b* :

306.

307.

To close, we present an example of a more extended problem:

308.

Those indications will be sufficient to enable us to form for ourselves manifold problems.

PART III.

PRACTICAL APPLICATION OF THE HARMONIES. –THE EXERCISES IN THEIR USE IN THE PURE HARMONIC STRUCTURE.

THROUGH the following hints respecting the manner most to the purpose in the use of the harmonies, the principles until now developed will be, at the same time, still more exactly explained, extended, and made complete. To this end, individual cases will furnish opportunity for farther remarks.

CHAPTER XVII.

The Simply Harmonic Accompaniment to a Given Voice.

IT may first be remarked, that here, only *simply melodic progression* of a voice will be discussed; all other elements of a melody, as, for example, its metrical and rythmical development, will be for the present excluded.

1. *Harmonic accompaniment to a Soprano.*
We select the following simple *exercise :*

309.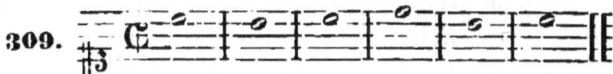

To facilitate the work, those fundamental tones, which can serve as the harmonic foundation, will be added in the manner used before.

310.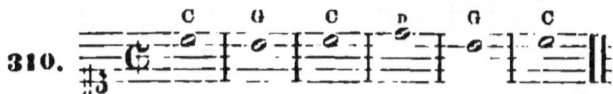

With every harmonic progression, the leading of the Bass is the most important point.

We turn our attention therefore first to this, and write its progression perhaps, in the following manner :

311.

or in the following way:

312.

The addition of the middle voices will now present no difficulties

313.

Let this working out of the exercise serve, for the present, for the explanation of the exercises themselves.

The next exercises will give opportunity for becoming acquainted with the principles of a good leading of the Bass, as well as of melodic voices in general so far as the simplest harmonic progression requires.

Examples worked out in a faulty manner can best serve this end.

Exercise with indication of the fundamentals:

314.

REMARK.—In the treatment of this and the following examples we use the violin clef for the sake of saving room, and write the voices together on two staves; for the personal work of the pupil, however, we recommend most earnestly, the manner of notation used in No. 313.

The working out of this exercise may be as follows:

315.

There appears nowhere in this example a transgression of any rule of progression and chord-connection thus far known, and still, on account of the stiff, uncertain, and powerless Bass, it is to be rejected entirely.

Except in the case of the organ-point, a good harmonic leading of the Bass allows it to remain stationary only if its continuity is conditioned by necessary preparation of a tone, or compensated for by a decided progression of the other voices.

The previous example also contains the *chord of the sixth and fourth* twice, which may give us opportunity to add what is farther necessary concerning the use of this peculiar and difficult chord.

Of the Use of the Chord of the Sixth and Fourth.

The rare use of the second inversion of the triad, the chord of th sixth and fourth, has its reason in this, that its appearance depends upon certain conditions.

First, we find it oftenest *in connection with the cadence-formations*, as former examples show.

Then, it appears in a like character *in connection with modulation.* (See page 143).

It can probably also enter free in both cases, it must then, however, be regarded not as a passing chord, but always *appear upon the thesis.*

Except in these cases, it appears most naturally as *tonic, dominant,* or *sub-dominant triad,* under the following conditions :

a.   *If the fourth is prepared ;*

b.   *If the Bass progresses by degrees to the following new chord, or remains stationary*

The following examples show the application :

316.

In the Examples at *a*, it appears most naturally, because it rests upon tonic, dominant and sub-dominant, while upon other degrees (*b*) it easily produces the feeling of a modulation.

Used upon the arsis (beside appearing under the above conditions), it can also appear with *preparation of the Bass*.

The chord of the sixth and fourth shows itself in all these examples, either as passing chord (upon the arsis), or, as above, in the character of the suspension upon the thesis; with preparation of the Bass upon the thesis, it appears much weaker.

Not unfrequently it will appear as itself a suspension, whereby the preparation of the fourth is perfectly justified.

In the second case still more decidedly, because it arises with a rarely occurring chord (that of the third degree).

That the chord of the sixth and fourth, however, can also enter free in connection with a leading, by degrees, of the voices of smaller measural divisions, in passing, as:

320.

will require no farther explanation after what was said in Chapter **XV.**, of the passing chords, and after the examples, Nos. 276, 279.

REMARK.—The often necessary preparation of the perfect fourth in the chord of the sixth and fourth, has led many theorists to reckon it among the dissonances.

In the introduction to this system of harmony, in the division of the intervals (page 16), it is introduced among the consonances; and also (page 20) the reason of this view is given.

The doubtful relation of the perfect fourth, and the necessity of its preparation occurs only *over against the Bass*, or the lowest voice, and, in fact, in the chord of the sixth and fourth only, since in the chord of the sixth, fourth and third, itself, this necessity of preparation is not always found; between the other voices the perfect fourth is to be treated just as any other consonance.

With the real dissonances this is not the case, for these retain their character everywhere, whether they appear above, below, or in the middle.

The chord of the sixth and fourth of the diminished triad will seldom be appropriate for use four-voiced, because it appears too incomplete.

321.

On the other hand, it will occur in three-voiced composition, where it often takes the place of the chord of the second. (See later, the three-voiced movement).

Besides the condition of a good harmonic progression, viz., that the Bass itself should form a good and intelligible foundation for it, the second requirement is,

THAT THE PROGRESSION SHOULD ALSO BE MELODIC.

Among the unmelodic progressions have always been rightly reckoned certain skips.

The succession of two fourths and fifths in the same direction, *e. g.*

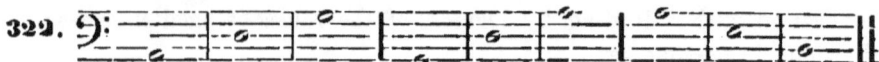

322.

These skips are improved thus:

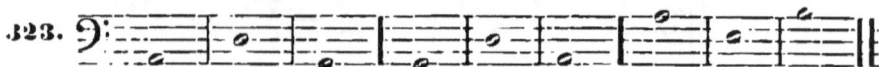

323.

Even skips of a sixth, if the situation and compass of the voices admits of it, are better carried out by skips of a third in a contrary movement:

324.   *better:*   *better:*

Augmented interval-steps and skips are to be avoided as unmelodic; diminished are, however, good.

325.   *not:*   *better:*   *not:*   *better:*

not: *better:*   *not:*   *better:*

Deviations from this rule are often found; they find their explanation in a formation of melody, or in the especial character of the composition as a whole. The observance of the rule in theoretical labors will always be very improving.

The skip into the major seventh is to be entirely avoided; that into the minor seventh can be used, but only in case of an inversion of the same chord.

326.   *not:*   *not:*

The last, perhaps, with the following progression of harmony:

327.   *not very good:*   *not:*   *not:*

These few observations contain the *principal features* of a good
melodic leading of the voices, and especially for the next (simply harmonic)
exercises, prove themselves sufficient. It should still be remarked, that
these rules apply, not alone for the leading of the Bass, but in general for
all voices.

The exercise given under No. 314 can, with an improved progression of
the Bass, be worked out something in this manner:

Exercises.

The next example will give occasion for the explanation of an impor
tant and difficult part of harmonic connection and leading of voices.

Exercise.

The following faulty work may serve for illustration:

The faults of this treatment of the exercise consist, firstly, in the doubling of the third of the second chord through the Bass, which, without occasion, gives to this and the following harmony an awkward position; secondly, in the indicated covered fifth (from the fourth to the fifth measure), and lastly, in the introduction of the seventh by a skip, in the next to the last measure.

As concerns the last, this can take place with the dominant seventh only—the fundamental being already present (prepared).   (See page 70).

More tolerable and less harsh is the free entrance of the seventh, and of the fundamental in *contrary motion ;*

in *parallel motion,* however, it is either to be rejected entirely, or only applied in connection with especially favorable progressions, if, perhaps, as in the first example of No. 333, the fundamental (G) is already present in the previous chord, although in another voice.

The first of the faults instanced above will be corrected in what follows. The second is more important, and will give us occasion to speak in general

OF COVERED FIFTH AND OCTAVE PROGRESSIONS.

The nature of these progressions has already been spoken of, page 29.

Covered fifths and octaves arise, *if two voices, starting with different intervals, progress* IN PARALLEL MOTION *to an octave or fifth, e. g.*

These fifths and octaves become open, if the skip which one or both voices make, be filled out by the tones which lie between, as is indicated above by the points.

Since in every four-voiced movement certain covered fifths and octaves can occur, without which the choice of chords, as well as the eading of the voices, would be very much limited, and also, since others are to be avoided, it becomes necessary to take a somewhat nearer view of the *manner* of their appearance. An attempt to give positive rules for their use, which would be sufficient for all cases, has not yet been success-ful, and would probably with great difficulty succeed; there are, therefore, only general observations to be made, which, however, will furnish a stan-dard of criticism for especial cases.

Covered fifths and octaves between two voices can occur:

1. *If one voice moves by a step and the other skips;*
2. *If both voices skip.*

In the first case:

a. *By a step in the upper, and a skip in the lower voice;*
b. *By a skip in the upper, and a step in the lower voice.*

In regard to both cases as concerns the kind of voices:

a. Between the *outer voices,*
b. Between the *middle voices,* and
c. Between an *outer* and a *middle voice.*

Covered Fifths and Octaves in the Outer Voices..

They are to be allowed, *if the upper voice progresses by a step.*

Here it is well, if one voice be at the same time led in the contrar movement or remain stationary, as in Example No. 335 *a, b, c.* It i not so well, if all voices go in parallel motion (*d*).

REMARK.—Although the above rule will suffice in so many cases, still it cannot al rays apply, as the above Example, No. 335 *d,* shows, which is not to be reckoned among those which exhibit a first rate leading of the voices, since the progression fi in the chord of the sixth, *c,* is a very forced one.

We must remember also, what has been said before concerning the cadencing pro gression of the Bass, pages 35 and 36, viz., that covered octaves which pass over the *leading tone,* or in general, over the *half-step,* are always more tolerable than those which pass over the whole step.

In the exercises exhibited above, the octave always shows itself as *fundamental* of the chord ; cases in which it forms the third of the chord are much more questionable, and therefore to be used more cautiously.

336.

Even as fifth of the chord it is not to be called **good**.

337.

REMARK.—With the covered fifth, the *lower voice* will always be the fundamental o the chord.

Covered fifths in the outer voices are to be rejected if the upper voice skips.

338.

Wherever a seventh makes the connection of the harmony firmer, as at *b, d, e,* the progression of fifths appears more covered and less harsh.

Covered octaves in the outer voices are not to be unconditionally rejected if the upper voice skips.

339.

Here also those cases in which the Bass progresses a half-step (*a*) show themselves to be most tolerable. What was said in connection with Nos 336 and 337 applies for *d* and *e.*

Covered fifths and octaves in the outer voices are to be rejected if both voices skip.

240.

If, however, *they only form inversions of the same chord*, they are not to be considered as faults, since in that case they are not *progressing fifths and octaves at all.*

341.

Covered Fifths and Octaves in the Middle Voices.

Although the leading of the middle voices must be just as pure as that of the outer, still their situation, which is much covered by the latter allows them occasionally a greater freedom; this particularly applies to the covered fifths. Covered octaves are, here, if only for the sake of the good relation of the voices, not to be called good; with respect to the covered fifths, aside from the above observations, all will immediately depend upon an otherwise good connection of harmony. A few cases may have place here:

342.

Covered Fifths and Octaves between the Outer and Middle Voices.

The considerations which are to be taken into account in connection with these progressions of the voices, are to be sought in a good and natural connection of harmony, rather than established through merely mechanical rules. Here are some examples:

313.

not good: not:

An especial kind of covered octaves is still to be mentioned, viz., such as pass *over the seventh;* these, in all voices, are to be avoided as faulty.

314.

(See page 84.)

That which was remarked of the octaves, applies also to *covered unisons.* Between Soprano, Alto and Tenor, the latter are to be avoided entirely, between Tenor and Bass, however, they are to be regarded as covered octaves—according to the position of the chord and of the voices themselves.

The cases, in which covered fifths and octaves can appear, are so manifold, that it would be superfluous, if it were, in fact, possible, to adduce them all. The above observations may suffice, if we add the following maxim, which, to be sure, is not written for those beginners who still have to do with the technical, or the properly mechanically-harmonic structure, without regarding the higher requirements of art:

Avoid, indeed, covered fifths and octaves as much as possible; consider them, however, as safe if on the one hand, an otherwise natural, good connection of harmony takes place, or on the other, considerations of a higher sort prevail; such as melodic voice-movement, application of definite motives. etc.

After this digression, we return to No. 330, in order to correct the before-mentioned fault.

A correction of the covered fifth found there, which belongs in that category where both voices skip, will be hardly possible in this case, because, even if the Bass-progression proceed in the contrary movement, the evil presents itself again in another place, *e. g.*

Thus it only remains to alter, in this case, the harmony itself, and select another marking of the fundamental tones.

The following alteration can take place:

or :

Exercises.

The following exercise:

348.

we will work out in this manner:

349.

The faults of this work are indicated by figures.

The movement of all the upper three voices, by skips in parallel motion, at No. 1, is not good, since it offends against the first principles of all harmonic connection and is by no means necessary.

A leading of one or two voices, by skips, can take place only if through a third voice (by a tone remaining stationary or by a contrary motion), the harmonic connection is preserved.

No. 2 also contains the same fault, which here becomes still harsher because seventh and fundamental enter *free* and come thereby into an awkward position, so that one is crowded by the other.

It has already been mentioned (pages 72 and 158), that the free entrance of the seventh can take only place without harshness, if the fundamental is already present, and can remain stationary in the same voice.

Thus, none of the following *examples* exhibit a superior leading of the voices.

350.

Probably few of these and similar instances would be excusable for more important melodic reasons.

The following *examples* may still serve as completion of the free introduction of the fundamental and the seventh in contrary motion, mentioned on page 158.

The instance No. 2, of Example No. 349, contains besides this, another fault, contrary to the rule laid down above (page 153), in connection with the chord of the sixth and fourth, viz., that the Bass should not skip from the chord of the sixth and fourth.

The third fault of Example No. 349 consists in the covered fifth, which is the more prominent in connection with the skip of the Soprano in the same direction, as well as in the general scattered leading of the voices.

The covered fifth in No. 4 is to be condemned, on the ground that it was not necessary; that at No. 5 is better; it can take place in connection with the leading of the Alto, as well as of the Bass in contrary motion.

The following will be a better working out of Exercise No. 348.

Exercises.

The next *exercise,*

353.

with the following treatment:

354.

gives us opportunity to speak of a fault which bears the name,

UNHARMONIC CROSS-RELATION.

The unharmonic cross-relation (relatio non harmonica) belongs to the unmelodic progressions, and consists in general in this; *that upon one tone immediately follows the same tone* IN ANOTHER VOICE, *chromatically raised or depressed,* as here upon the G of the Alto the G♯ of the Bass.

In order to avoid this fault, note the following rule:

Immediate chromatic alterations of a tone are to be applied in that voice, alone in which the tone unaltered immediately before occurs.

Notwithstanding this rule answers, in so great degree, to all theoretical principles of harmonic connection and progression, there is hardly any one, to which so many exceptions in the practice can be shown.

For this reason, in the books of instruction of later methods, great suspicion has been cast upon the doctrine of the cross-relation, and instances brought forward in which the unharmonic cross relations occur in a perfectly natural manner, without examining the reason why they do not sound faulty.

Some of them will be here adduced:

255

In all these cases the cross relation appears, not formed through the *simply-harmonic leading forward* of the voices, but either

In the character of changing notes at a, b, g, or *through contraction* (drawing together) *of natural, but for the metrical construction, too circumstantial harmonic connections,* at *c, d, e, f, h.*

The first needs no proof, and there is only the observation to be added, that this kind of cross-relations would probably occur mostly with smaller divisions of the measure, and the above notation in half notes is rare and therefore unsuitable, because through it the simple *harmonic* foundation is expressed, and not those tonic elements, which serve for embellishment.

The original progression of the voices with the above cross-relations, which are the result of contraction, is the following:

Let these examples be compared with those under No. 355, at *c, d, e, h.*

Al. these conditions, through which cross-relations are most endurable
are wanting in the following and similar cases, which are therefore faulty

257.

In all the above instances, which are taken from practice, but separated from their connection, is still to be added the consideration of
the tempo, of the consistency of a whole brought out by means of rythmical divisions, which will make all these formations not unpleasant, but
rather, precise.

Among the cross-relations is reckoned also a progression which is known
under the name *Tritonus*, and the explanation of which follows here :

Of the Tritonus.

The tritonus is contained in the diatonic major scale, and embraces the
distance from the fourth to the seventh degree (in the C major scale *th
augmented fourth* F–B.)

This step from F to B embraces *three whole tone-steps*, whence its name
is derived :

358.

It is held to be unmelodic and unvocal because each of its tones requires
an especial progression, which tones properly appear assigned to two different voices :

359.

of which the one must remain disregarded in its progression, if the step
is transferred to *one* voice :

360.

unless the melodic succession be formed thus :

361.

That this, however, is not the only reason of the unpleasant effect of this interval-step, is shown by the very often used inversion of the same, which would likewise require a two voiced progression,

362.

and is just as intelligible and easy of performance, as the tritonus appears difficult and refractory.

REMARK.—It may still be remarked, in this connection, that the tritonus depends upon the diminished triad and its progression, as becomes plain from Example No. 362 above. (See page 38).

That this step was formerly especially held up as faulty, lay in the circumstance, that, in connection with the otherwise customary simple harmonic formation of tone-compositions, it formed the only *augmented* progression which diatonically exhibited itself. At this day, with the extended use of all artistic means, it is simply reckoned among the augmented progressions, which, in a *pure* harmonic leading of the voices, are to be avoided as unmelodic, or at least, used with caution.

The things to which reference is to be had in the use of the tritonus, are its situation and its manner of appearance.

It can occur, based either

Upon *one chord* (*a*) or

Upon *two chords* (*b*), *e. g.*

363. *a.*   *b.*

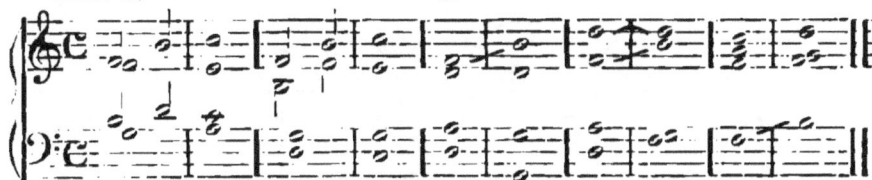

If it occurs upon one chord, its entrance is not unexpected, and the ear is prepared; in connection with two chords, however, the feeling of a forced progression is easily produced.

Formerly the prohibition of the tritonus was extended to the *two major thirds*, which follow each other at the distance of a *whole* step, *e. g.*,

not however:

364.

and it is not to be denied, that this progression produces, *two-voiced*, the same unpleasant effect, whereas the same three and four-voiced, especially if it does not appear in the outer voices, is rendered much milder.

365.

That formerly the step from the fourth to the seventh degree of the minor scale, e. g., D to G♯, was not reckoned as tritonus, is founded upon the former usual representation of the minor scale itself, and its harmonies. The effect of this step, since it is augmented, remains the same.

We return again to our Exercise No. 353, and attempt a better treatment.

366.

Exercises.

366 b.

2. *Harmonic accompaniment to a given middle voice.*

This exercise, which belongs properly to the contrapuntal labors, cannot begin too early. It is introduced, for the present, with the addition of the fundamentals.

Exercise.

In the treatment of this exercise, the first and most important thing will, again, be the sketching of the Bass. At the same time, however, the Soprano, as the most prominent voice, can be added, *e. g.*

The foregoing can answer as a three-voiced movement; through the addition of the Tenor it will assume this form:

Exercises with given Alto.

6.

A Tenor voice would be treated in like manner.

Exercise.

370.

Sketch of the Bass and Soprano:

371.

Four-voiced:

372.

Exercises with given Tenor.

372 b.

These exercises are to be continued, until the sketching of the Bass, as well as the leading of the voices in general, is perfectly pure and certain.

At the close of this chapter it should be remarked, that to a good carrying out of these four-voiced movements, a good position of the voices is especially necessary; the boundaries of the voices themselves must not be overstepped, the distance from one voice to the other must not be too great, neither must it be too small; this, however, does not apply to two voices, which, for example, meet upon one tone.

In this relation let the following rule be noted:

Of the upper three voices, the distance from one to the next must not be greater than one octave. The relation of the Bass to the Tenor, however, admits of exceptions.

REMARK.—To set the present exercises in the Bass, will not be to the purpose since they would appear exactly in the former manner, as figured Basses. They can only be set for *free* harmonic treatment.

CHAPTER XVIII.

Extension of the Harmonic Accompaniment.

To a given voice in whole notes, the harmonic accompaniment in half-notes interchangeably in the other voices. This can take place,

Through *two* chords,
Through *change of the situation of one chord,*
Through *suspensions.*

The exercises will be marked in the same manner as heretofore.

Exercise.

373.

The Bass can be sketched in this manner:

374.

In the second and fourth measures, sevenths of secondary chords of the seventh show themselves without preparation.

Tl.s kind are called *passing sevenths*. They start from the fun lamenta. of the chord, and always appear upon the *arsis*. In such a manner they can occur in all voices.

The addition of the middle voices to the above sketch of a Bass, gives the following four-voiced movement.

375.

2   6   7   2   6   8   7

The same exercise with a richer change of harmony can be given in this manner:

376.

C   F rʒ⁰₇   G eʒ⁰₇   ▲C₇♭   ᴅD   G—₇   C

Treatment:

377.

6   7♭   7   4   6   —   8   7
                              3♭

The next exercise will exhibit the use of the suspensions.

378.

F   B♭   C   ᴅ   ɢ   F   B♭   C₇   F

Treatment:

379.

9   8   5   —   9

We pass over the exercises in the middle voices.

The using of the simply melodic progression in whole notes, as exercises, (cantus firmus) took place for this purpose, viz., in order to exhibit the simple harmonic content of a measure, or, as takes place in Alla-breve measure, to exhibit it in its principal divisions (half-notes). If the exercise is given in half-notes, then chorals can be selected for the purpose.

For personal practice the fundamental tones of existing good harmonic treatments of chorals can be very easily drawn off, and the treatment attempted.

In the next exercise the process will be be shown.

Choral: O Haupt voll Blut und Wunden.

The treatment of this choral can, according to the above exercise, b the following:

After sufficient practice and certainty in the management of the simple harmony, we can proceed to a farther development of the leading of the voices, by means of the passing and changing notes.

For this purpose will follow in the next chapter the farther discussion of melody and melodic progression.

CHAPTER XIX.

On the Development of Melody.

WE are not to treat here of the invention of a melody, but of its development, and, what is most important for our harmonic exercises, to treat of it in order to learn, by the elaboration and fashioning of melodies, to know and use what in them is essentially harmonic.

All will here depend upon the recognition and comprehension of the following principles:

Every melody, however extended and developed it may be, has a founda tion just as simple as those we have used, as exercises, in our last examples

Every harmonic leading of the voices, however complicated, admits, therefore, of reduction to a simple connection of harmony.

In order to recognize this, it is necessary to learn to distinguish the essential notes from the subordinate and accessory work.

We select to this end the analytic method, and endeavor to develop the following melody, which we will write down in the simplest manner according to the above mode with indication of the fundamental tones.

Both melody and harmony are, as selected, simple, and the latter may be carried out, four-voiced, in the following manner :

Before we proceed to a farther development of this movement, it becomes necessary to premise what is to be mentioned concerning the rythmical formation of a melody.

A melody can be either a musical movement without definite boundary containing more or less measures, as it is often found as theme (motive of a composition), or it can be a whole, separated and bounded by means of ntitheses.

In the last case it is called a Period, and it contains then, as a rule eight measures, which, in two divisions, each of four measures, form antitheses. These antitheses or divisions are often called " thesis and anti thesis " (Vordersatz und Nachsatz).

The more complete treatment of this subject belongs to the doctrine of Form.*

That the above movement will form a period, is seen in the close of the whole, and it will be necessary, above all, to seek out the separating point of the divisions.

This point of separation is very often discovered in the cadences, which either as imperfect whole or as half-cadences, show themselves as plagal in the middle of the movement.

Such a *half-cadence* (in general, a close in the dominant) is found in our exercise in the sixth and seventh measures, and the separating point of the divisions of the periods may be assumed to be at the place where the sign † stands.

The first division, the thesis, would accordingly receive *seven*, the antithesis *six* measures, each of which can be rythmically altered so as to contain four measures. This may take place in the following manner:

384.

If we add the harmonic accompaniment selected above, we obtain a complete musical period.

It needs, also, only a glance, to enable us to see that all farther transformations into various kinds of measure, e. g., into $\frac{2}{4}$, $\frac{3}{4}$, $\frac{3}{8}$ or $\frac{6}{8}$ measure, admit of easy accomplishment, e. g.

385.

&c.

&c.

&c.

We proceed now to the tonic variations of the melody, and add to it passing and changing notes, e. g.

386.

* See the work of this author—" *Die Grundzüge der musikalischen Formen.*"—(Leipsic, G. Wigand.)

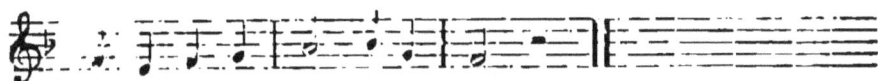

Still richer use of all by-tones could give the following turnation:

387.

Adagio.

Originally:

The simple melodic progression found below, will be easily recognized as the fundamental voice. That, however, the above melody is carried out with reference to the original harmony, will immediately become evident, if we add the other voices with the few deviations conditioned by the upper voice:

388.

Adagio.

p

We may remark concerning the octave parallels in the middle voices, to be found in the third measure of this example, that they are to be regarded as faultless if they do not occur singly, but appear only as a means of additional strength, in a more extended succession, for the intensification of a harmonic and melodic progression. The movement is, in this case, to be regarded as three-voiced.

As little independent worth as this example has, it still served, here, to show of what development the simplest melodic and harmonic movement is capable.

The advantage of the contemplation and recognition of these melodic and harmonic relations is too great to allow us to forbear to furnish another example in the following interesting movement.

The fundamental harmonic progression is just as simple as that shown efore.

389.

This movement forms a period; the middle close is easily found in the half-cadence of the seventh measure.

We omit here the various kinds of measure, and select the following division:

390

The development of the upper voice may take place in the following manner reference being had to the harmonic progression :

391.

What part the other voices can take in melodic development, the following movement from the E♭ major quartette of Beethoven will show:

392.

Adagio.

VIOLINO I.

VIOLINO II.

VIOLA

VIOLONCELLO.

A comparison with No. 390 will show the melodic and harmonic variations.

There now follows still another alteration of the original melody, out of the same composition :

393.

The other voices show themselves in the following alteration:

394.

These hints in reference to melodic development may, here, suffice, and be left to personal practice or special guidance.

REMARK.—The mechanical element in the whole proceeding should not occasion mistake; for just so certain as it is that in composition one does not always proceed in the way shown above (even if Beethoven, in the later alterations of these original melodies, could not, sometimes, proceed otherwise), in even so great a degree was it here our only object, partly, to set in the right light the relation of our previous exercises to the practical side, and partly, to gain a clear insight into complicated compositions themselves.

As concerns the accompanying voices, they arose of themselves out of the simple manner of harmonizing, required little alteration, and showed themselves, even if subordinate, still not on that account insignificant.

It yet remains to speak concerning other kinds of accompaniment, which will be done in the next chapter

CHAPTER XX.

On Development of the Accompanying Voices.

THE last examples of the foregoing chapter have already shown in what manner the accompanying voices take part in harmonic, metrical and melodic development.

There are, however, still other kinds of accompaniment, which are known under the name of

THE FIGURATED ACCOMPANIMENT.

This is not adapted to the character of the vocal parts, and may be used for them only in a very limited manner. In the following investigation, instrumental music only will be treated of.

By figurated accompaniment is understood the kind of accompaniment arising through metrically uniform transformation of the simple chord tones, *e. g.*

The accompaniment at *a* is *harmonically figurated.* The figures arising therefrom are called also *broken chords.* That at *b* is *metrically figurated*, and that at *c* is *melodically figurated.* The figures which have arisen from the last are formed from changing and passing notes.

Any accompanying voice can be used for such figuration, either alone or in connection with other voices.

We select the beginning of Example No. 382, in order to attempt some kinds of accompaniment.

This may be preceded by the following remarks:

If the figures repeat themselves uniformly (e. g. in broken chords), *then*

all the rules of the harmonic leading of the voices are to be observed at the CHANGE OF THE CHORDS, *as well as in the reduplication.*

We must not write:

but somewhat in this manner:

At the change of the harmony, the *last note* of one figure and the *first note* of the next must not form a false progression with any other voice, *e. g.*

The harmonic figuration also affords the means for forming *one-voiced movements* in greater perfection. The examples will begin with this:

That these movements are calculated for an instrument, probably such as a violin or clarionet, is easy to be seen.

100.   *Two voiced:*

Three voiced:
In the middle voices: **In the lower voice:**

In the upper voice:

In two voices:

The figuration in the four-voiced movement, after these attempts with the above example, will be equally easy of accomplishment.

Instead of this we prefer to select, as an example of manifold figuration, the following passage from the above quoted quartette movement of Beethoven.

101.

This whole rich development rests upon the foundation given in **Nos.** 390, 391 and 392, and wherever the harmonic change enters, the leading of the voices is carefully observed.

If we wish to obtain a clear insight into such elaborated compositions, and arrive at an understanding of their inner harmonic structure, it will be very useful to reduce compositions of this kind back to their simple foundation; industry in this will reward itself by enrichment of knowledge of many kinds, and by our being rendered capable of **formations of our own.**

CHAPTER XXI.

The Exercises in the Three-voiced Movement.

With few exceptions, the four-voiced form of writing has been used for our exercises hitherto, and although it affords greater completeness, and appears most adapted for the harmonic connections, the three-voiced movements are also of much advantage, since they are especially calculated to make the leading of the voices more skillful and many-sided.

We begin, as before, with the problems with figured Basses.

The three-voiced movement is sufficient, indeed, for the triad, but the leading of the voices will often result in the omission of one of its intervals; in the case of the chords of the seventh one interval must naturally always be wanting; this, however, can never be the seventh itself. As a rule, the fifth can be omitted, as has already occurred in the four-voiced movement, and the fundamental also in many cases; the third, as the interval which determines the mode, can only be omitted in a few cases, without producing an especial emptiness.

The treatment of the exercise is the following, to which a few remarks will be added :

In the fourth measure is found, at NB., the chord of the sixth and fourth of the diminished triad, F–G–B♭. It stands instead of the chord of the second, B♭–C–E–G, of which the fundamental C is here omitted. For **four** voices, this place would stand thus :

Concerning this chord, compare what is mentioned page 155.

In the fifth measure a fourth represents the chord. Now, although a fourth can neither in the three-voiced nor in the two-voiced movement have the worth of a complete chord, as can the third and sixth, yet, in cases where the chord of the sixth and fourth as *passing chord* can be used upon the arsis in the four-voiced movement, probably the sixth or third of the fundamental chord can (for the sake of a better lead ing of the voices) be omitted in the three-voiced, so that the fourth alone remains, marking, here, fundamental and fifth of the original chord.

In the two-voiced movement, the fourth will occasionally take the place of the chord of the second, especially in the case of the passing seventh, *e. g.*

Four-voiced, the above place in Example No. 403 would, complete, stand thus:

In the eighth measure of Example No. 403, the chord of the **sixth,** fourth and third is, by the skip of the Alto, formed complete.

The tenth measure exhibits apparently a chord of the sixth and fifth. Fundamentally, the fifth here is nothing else than the suspension of the fourth, which here, however, through the progression of the Bass, becomes a third. Four-voiced this becomes plainer :

407.

The closing measure of Example No. 403 shows, through the octave f, that the triad can appear, in such cases, even without third and fifth.

That the omission of the third is often conditioned by the leading of the voices, is shown by the first and second measures of the next example.

408.

The omission of the third takes place best upon the arsis, as here in the last measural division; upon the thesis, (accordingly at the beginning of the measure), the third should not be wanting.

Farther exercises are to be left to the especial guidance [of the teacher]

Exercises in the Three-voiced Movement to a given Upper Voice.

The following exercise, with indication of the fundamental tones is to be worked out three-voiced:

This treatment needs no explanation.

The choice of the middle and lower voices will depend upon the position of the chords in general. Thus, in a low position, the Tenor as middle voice, will be more suitable than the Alto, just so the Tenor can be selected as lower voice instead of the Bass.

For the following example the Tenor is selected as middle voice, since its movement attaches itself more to the Bass, while on the other hand the simple song of the Soprano appears, of itself, isolated.

The previous *Exercise* in more extended harmonic treatment:

In the fifth measure at NB. appears the real ninth-suspension (through the position of the voices), as second, which occurs very seldom, and only between Tenor and Bass. In this connection it is to be remarked, that a second-suspension cannot exist, because the second depends upon the inversion of the seventh, and governs itself according to the progression of the latter, *e. g*

113.

Exercise in a middle voice.

114.

As upper voice, the selection of the Alto is here most to the purpose.

115.

The same *Exercise* with the following determination of chords:

116

Treatment:

117.

The next to the last measure affords the proof, that even the sixth can be suspension.

For farther practice, former exercises, which were given for the four-voiced movement, may be used.

CHAPTER XXII.

On the Two-voiced Movement.

THE great meagreness of the two-voiced movement, in a purely harmonic point of view, allows it rarely to appear adapted for other than contrapuntal labors, in which it first receives actual significance and comes to be applied even in polyphonic movements, *e. g.*, in fugues.

If, indeed, for simply harmonic use, the metrically and rhythmically various formation of the voices makes the two-voiced movement tolerable, still the contrapuntal development of two voices can alone free them from the monotony of many successions of thirds and sixths, and give this movement that individual completeness, which every other polyphonic movement must possess.

The omission of one or more intervals will, in every case, necessarily take place in connection with this movement. With the triads, it will generally be the fifth or the fundamental. If chords of the seventh are to be applied, then, of course, the seventh cannot be omitted. Octaves and fifths are seldom to be introduced, since they appear too empty; the fourth could only be admitted in a few cases where the chord of the sixth and fourth can regularly stand, or if it occurs instead of the chord of the second. (See page 188).

Example:

418.

Treatment:

419.

The omission of intervals is plain through a comparison of the fun
lamental tones of Example No. 418. Want of clearness of the harmony
will be rare in connection with this, since each chord explains itself through
its situation, *i. e.*, through the preceding and following harmony.

The same exercise with the following marking:

Most of the exercises exhibited in the third part trespass upon the
domain of counterpoint. The difference consists only in this, viz.; that here,
the succession of the chords is prescribed, and it only remains to form the
leading of the voices, while in the contrapuntal exercises the knowledge of
harmony, as well as certainty in its use, is assumed, so that the succession of the harmonies can be left to our own choice.

We may, therefore, regard these labors as a useful preparatory exercise
for those, as they also afford at the same time an insight into the relation
of harmony to counterpoint.

The exercises in the next chapter are also to be considered in this light,
since they drop the above limitation of a prescribed succession of chords.

CHAPTER XXIII.

Harmonic Elaboration of a given Voice in Melodic Develop ment.

By melodic development of a voice is not here to be understood that richer ornamentation, such as Chapter XIX. exhibited. Through metrical variety of their measural-divisions alone the simple, choral-like progression of our earlier exercises will be avoided, and thereby opportunity be given to learn to develop better the voices of the harmonic accompaniment also.

The following exercise will make this plainer:

422.

The choice of the chord-succession is left to the treatment itself.

Even if the kind of measure selected will, of itself, produce a like melodic leading of the voices to be elaborated, still especial attention must be given to a good leading of them, according to the principles developed .n the previous chapters, if a free, skillful treatment of them is to be attaine l.

This exercise will follow, first in three-voiced treatment.

423.

This treatment, after what has been remarked in connection with the three-voiced movemen* needs no farther explanation.

The harmonic treatment of this melody as middle voice will show its many-sidedness, and may be recommended as a useful exercise.

In order to be able to retain the Alto voice, we transpose the melody, for the sake of the better position, to F major.

424.

The explanation of the chord of the sixth and fourth which enters free in the fourth measure, is found in what was remarked in Chapter XV. concerning the passing chords. It arose accidentally, through the progression of the Bass by degrees, and stands, here, in the place of the chord of the second.

The treatment of the same *cantus firmus* transferred to the Bass:

425.

This treatment exhibits a weakness in the third and fourth measures, in the harmonizing of the sustained A of the Bass. In like manner the bare fourth in the sixth measure is a very imperfect representative of a chord, unless we wish to explain it as a passing note.

If we wish to develop the leading of the voices still farther, we can introduce passing and changing notes interchangeably, into the two voices to be added, *e. g.*

126.

Of the remaining treatments, that of the *cantus firmus* in the middle voices will here be given:

As examples of four-voiced treatment, the following may stand here:

428 *Given voice:*

429. *Four-voiced treatment:*

In the fifth measure, at NB., the skip of the Tenor into the seventh is not good, because the Soprano, at the same time, makes a long skip in the same direction, into the fundamental G; only the position of the Alto can excuse this case.

In the same measure is found the chord of the sixth and fourth of the augmented triad, the original fifth of which is prepared (pages 91 and 92). It stands here in the character of a suspension from below. (See Suspensions, Chap. XII., page 116).

The same *cantus firmus* in the Alto, transposed to D major:

430.

In the fourth measure are found suspensions in three voices (see page 117). In the fifth and sixth measures the position of the Alto and Tenor is not good, because the distance from one to the other is more than an octave.

Of the remaining treatments, that of the *cantus firmus* in the Bass will here follow:

The introduction of the chord of the seventh of the seventh degree, in the fourth measure, is not clear, because the fundamental lies immediately above the seventh. (See page 69).

Besides this, its progression does not ensue here according to the leading of the leading tone, but in the same cadencing manner as with the other chords of the seventh: C♯ °₇ F♯. (See pages 68 and 69).

The treatments of this *cantus firmus* with a leading of the voices in which there is more movement, can be carried out in this manner:

The upward progression of the seventh in the next to the last measure (at NB.), is conditioned by the movement of the Soprano.   (See page 84)

The treatment of the *cantus firmus* in the Tenor follows:

The third measure gives opportunity to speak of octave and fifth-succession *in contrary motion.*

According to the principle developed on page 27 and the following pages, they are just as faulty as those of the parallel motion, and it is to be especially remarked in connection with octave-successions, that they confine the free movement of the voices; with the fifth-successions, however, the character of separation is rendered much milder by contrary motion; this is particularly true of those which approach each other while those which progress *from* each other, make the separation or want of connection more perceptible. (See also **Example No. 430** in the 6th and 7th measures, between Tenor and Bass).

Compare the following examples:

431.

If we glance at the treatments found in this chapter, we cannot fail to recognize the melodic development of the voices, and herein lies the ground for regarding them as contrapuntal labors; for exactly in this consists the essence of counterpoint, in distinction from the purely rhythmical-harmonic form, viz., that it conditions the freer melodic leading of the voices, but with observance of the harmonic laws, which latter form, as it were, its innermost substance.

Everywhere now in these examples, even in those where the voices move in quarter notes, the simply harmonic structure can be demonstrated, and thus they may serve the purpose, for the present, of making us understand the difference between simply harmonic and contrapuntal treatment of a given voice. The more particular discussion of this can only be taken up in connection with counterpoint itself.

CHAPTER XXIV.

The Five-voiced Movement.

As the doubling of the intervals of a triad is necessary even in the four-voiced movement, so in five and more than five-voiced movements it becomes a necessity in a still greater degree, and this even in the case of the chords of the seventh.

Since in the pure harmonic movement, each voice must maintain its independence, those intervals especially which admit of a double progression, will, for the sake of attaining this independence, be capable of a reduplication. This, to be sure, can take place with each interval of a chord under certain circumstances; the seventh will be least adapted for doubling, except where a melodic leading, as, for example, in passing, renders this reduplication necessary.

Farther remarks follow in connection with the examples given.

Exercise.

435.

In the treatment, we can select, according to the position of the voices, either two Sopranos, two Altos or two Tenors.

436.

The same exercise carried out in another manner :

437.

It pertains also to the independence of the voices, that two voices de not remain stationary upon one tone or in the octave, *if the chords change.* In the above example, this is the case in the first and second measures between the second Soprano and Tenor, but here is not faulty, because he same chord only leaves its position, but is exchanged for no other.

The following case, however :

438.

would be corrected thus :

439.

REMARK.—This rule admits, however of frequent exceptions in connection with poly. phonic movements, because there other relations present themselves.

That the leading of the voices will also admit of the doubling of the leading tone, is shown by the third measure of Example No. 437, between the second Soprano and Tenor.

As in the four-voiced movement, so here in a still greater degree in the

five and more than five-voiced movement, the unavoidableness of covered
fifths, octaves and unisons will appear. That here also the *outer voices*
must progress in pure relations, and a greater freedom be allowed to the
middle voices only, may be mentioned again.

The following example contains various progressions of this sort:

The covered fifth, octave and unison progressions in this example are
indicated by strokes. The open fifth in the eighth measure between the
second Alto and Bass is not to be avoided, since *polyphonically* the chord
of the diminished seventh can, only with difficulty, be made to progress
otherwise.

The first and second Altos in the eighth and following measures could
also be made to progress thus:

441.

That the voices, particularly the middle voices, must often cross each other is shown by the second Alto and Tenor in the second and third measures.

For practice in the five-voiced movement, chorals especially can be used to advantage.

The following may be given here:

Choral: Allein Gott in der Höh' sei Ehr'.

442.

The work in the five and more than five-voiced movement requires a simple and natural Bass-progression, and the less artificial and difficult the latter, so much the clearer and more intelligible the succession of harmony itself will become; this is here the more important, since with the fullness of the chords and the necessity of the free movement of the voices, very unintelligible progressions can easily arise.

The beginning of this exercise follows here.

443.

In the repetition, the following succession of harmony can be applied

441.

CHAPTER XXV.

The Six, Seven and Eight-voiced Movement.

THE necessity of doubling or trebling increases with the number of the voices which are added; it will also often occur in connection with an independent leading of the voices, that the voices cross each other The simplest harmonic progressions become here, in a still greater degree, fundamental condition of the possibility of such polyphonic movements and it must be remarked, that many chords are not adapted at all for this manner of writing, because their intervals, in as much as they are subject to a definite progression, do not allow of multiplication, as, for example, the altered chords and the diminished chord of the seventh.

A few progressions of the triad may follow here.

Progression to the *second* degree:

445.

Progression to the *third* degree

Progression to the *fourth* degree:

Progression to the *fifth* degree:

We pass over farther combinations; to try them, with all inversions, will be of great use.

As example of the management of the leading of the voices, the choral found under No. 442, may follow here with six voices:

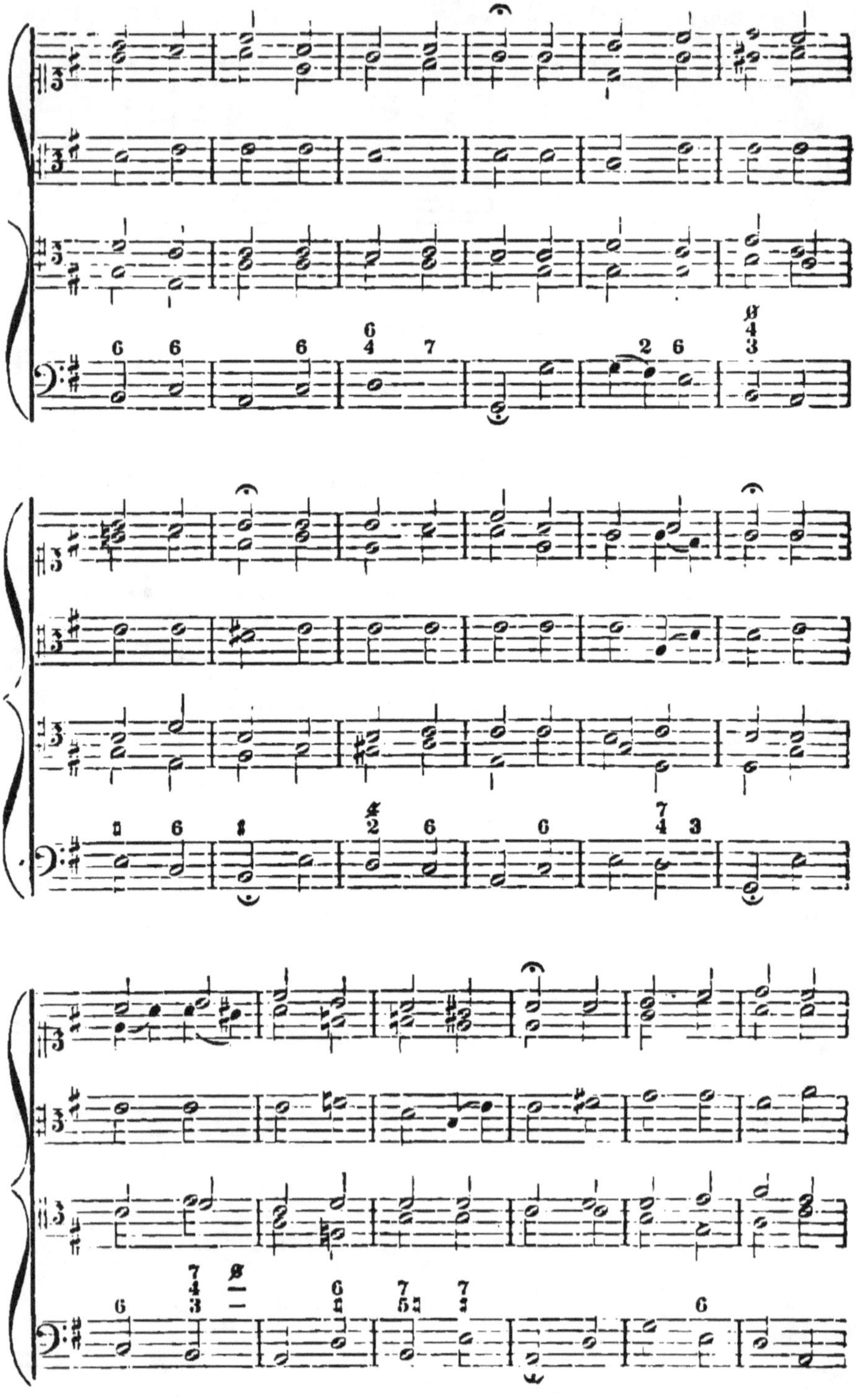

Since in polyphonic chorus-movements, all the voices do not always work at the same time, as in a choral-treatment, the movement often appears only three and four-voiced, and receives an increase of intensity through the accession of a number of voices.

The following examples will explain this kind of chorus-movement and especially serve to show, that in polyphonic work also, suspensions and passing notes can very well be introduced, without detriment to the clear ess and intelligibility.

447.

418.

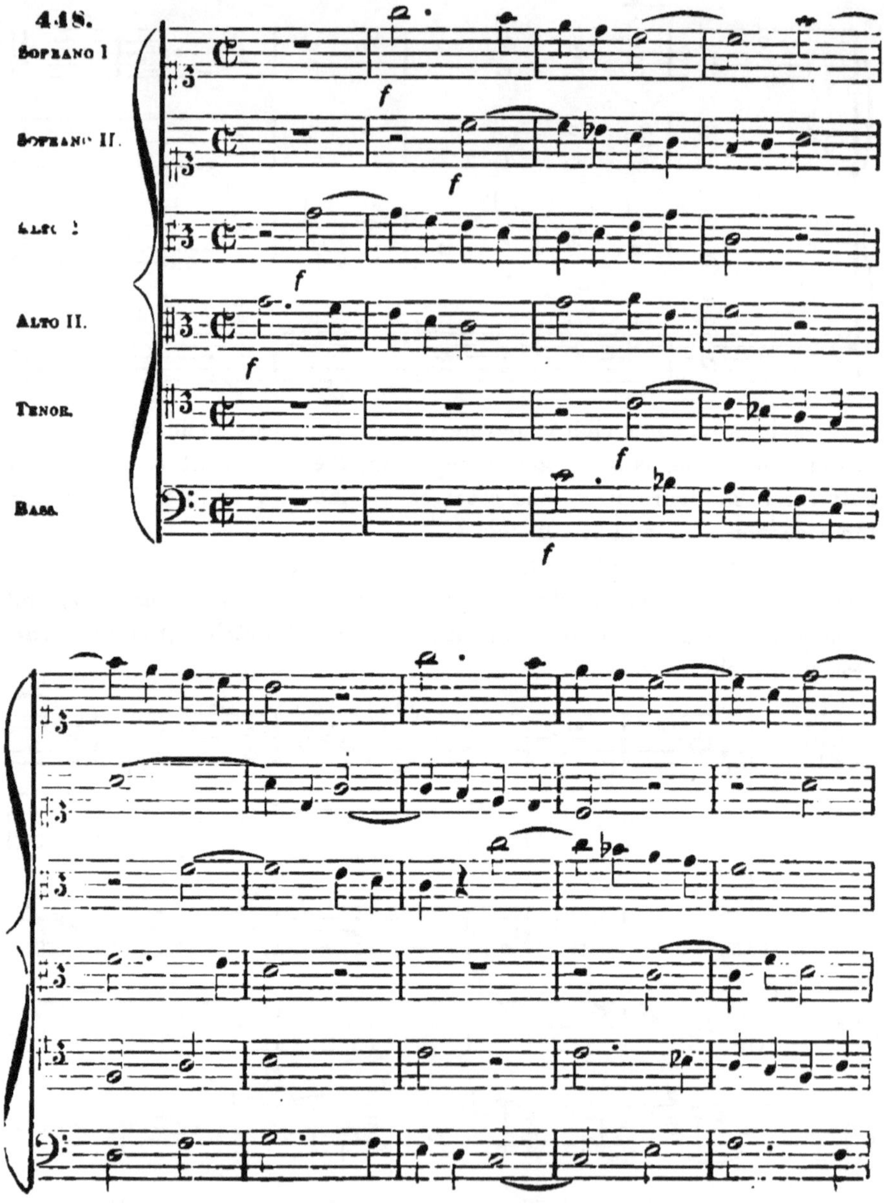

In eight-voiced chorus-movements, for which, as a rule, the customary four voices are used twice, the latter are not always found employed as eight independent voices, which would easily cause too great fullness, but frequently two voices of like kind are employed in unison (for example, two Sopranos, two Altos, or two Tenors and two Basses in unison), so that the movement often appears four, five and six-voiced. We find also the eight voices divided into two different choirs, which work each for itself, and only in single passages together.

As an example of the particular progression which many of these voices must make, the beginning of the choral given above may follow here for eight voices:

449.

Soprano I. & II.

Alto I. & II.

Tenor I. & II

Bass I & II.

The difficulty of this manner of writing is, in the case of polyphonic movements which are divided into two different choirs, met by this, that where two or more choirs work together, it is not altogether the *tonical* difference, but often the *metrical*, which separates the voices; it is always to be presumed, however, that the harmonic succession takes place in the simplest manner, and never in rapid changes.

The above is generally to be understood when we speak of twelve or sixteen-voiced choruses, movements, etc., and single pieces of *Bach* only are found, where eight and more voices (among which, however, instrumental voices are to be reckoned), are treated obligato.

These hints concerning the polyphonic movement may here suffice, since the rest, with thorough knowledge of harmony, can be left to personal study and the inclination for polyphonic movements. Concerning its application, however, we may farther remark that the use of the polyphonic form and its manner of treatment above shown, will have application mostly in compositions for choirs; in instrumental music. however e. *g.*, in orchestral works, will not find place (as the taking part of so many instruments of various kinds allows us to suppose) in the compass adduced for this last, in the majority of cases, the four-voiced movement will be sufficient, concerning the farther treatment of which only the *actual* instruction in instrumentation can give information, since here the relations of reduplication (even if often approaching the manner shown above), must still be subject to other principles.

JHAPTER XXVI.

On the Musical Forms of Close.

SEVERAL kinds of close have already been mentioned (pages 32 and 33), in relation to the authentic close, farther remarks followed on pages 40 and 53; in the course of the whole treatise, however, no farther opportunity has been given to take up the subject, so that a fuller explanation of these and other kinds of close may here follow:

The forms of close are immediately divided into

The *authentic close* and

The *plagalic* or *plagal close*.

The authentic close has the formula V–I, the plagal close IV–I (or in minor: V–ı, ıv–ı), as was before remarked.

Both kinds are used not only at the conclusions of whole compositions, but also at the close of the principal parts, of the periods, and their divisions. The more particular discussion of this point belongs to the doctrine of Form. (See the book referred to, page 142.)

If the plagal close concludes a piece, it seldom stands alone, but succeeds the authentic close; in a composition in minor it also frequently leads to major, *e. g.*

In the last case, as in the above example, it is introduced by means of a modulation.

The closes (cadences) are also divided into *whole* and *half* closes (cadences).

By the first is understood the same which is comprehended under the *authentic cadences*. In the case of the whole cadences a farther distinction is again made between *perfect* and *imperfect* ones.

The *perfect whole cadences* are those in which the Bass receives the

214 MANUAL OF HARMONY

fundamentals of the dominant and tonic, and the Soprano the fundamental of the tonic, e. g.

451.

If this is not the case, they are called *imperfect*, e. g.

452.

If the Bass progresses from the dominant to another degree, they are called *deceptive cadences*.

453.

See the examples, pages 82 to 85.
The *half-cadences* have the formula I–V, e. g.

454.

They consist therefore in this; that the *dominant* triad completes the movement.

Besides the tonic triad, other chords of other degrees can precede the dominant in the formation of a half-close, e. g.

455.

Among the *half-cadences* are also counted those closes in the *key of the dominant* which are formed by a modulation into the same; with which however, the modulation itself is not, in a definite manner, effected through the fundamental position of the dominant harmony of the seventh, but either through its inversions or through the chord of the seventh of the seventh degree, *e. g.*

This is, however, the case only in relation to the ruling key, which has immediately before been made use of.

For the farther understanding of these kinds of cadences, compare those which are found in the examples of this book.

In No. 388 is found in the third and fourth measures a *half* cadence formed through II–V, which effects the close of the first division of the whole period; in the seventh and eighth measures, however, we find a *perfect whole* or authentic cadence.

In Example No. 392 is found a half cadence, in the third and fourth measures, formed through I–V, and a *perfect whole* or *authentic* cadence in the key of the dominant at the conclusion. (Thus this is *no half* cadence, since the dominant harmony of the seventh renders the modulation decided).

In the choral treated under No. 446, the first strophe ends with an *imperfect whole* cadence, the second with a *perfect whole* cadence, the third with a *half*-cadence to E minor (IV–V), the fourth with a *perfect whole* cadence in G major, the fifth with a *perfect whole* cadence in A minor, the sixth with a *half* cadence in E minor (IV–V), and the seventh with a *perfect* whole cadence in G major.

The application of the various cadences is easily found in chorals; for more extended pieces they form the means of boundary and connection of the smallest, as well as of the more extended movements, and are therefore to be used with much care, because upon them depends a great part of the Form-construction of a piece.

www.ingramcontent.com/pod-product-compliance
Lightning Source LLC
Chambersburg PA
CBHW030822270326
41928CB00007B/857